REVISED, EXPANDED, UPDATED AND RE-TITLED SECOND EDITION

THE BEGINNER'S GUIDE TO

GRANT WRITING

TIPS, TOOLS & TEMPLATES TO WRITE WINNING GRANTS

HOLLY RUSTICK

HOST OF THE TOP-RANKED GRANT WRITING PODCAST

THE BEGINNER'S GUIDE TO GRANT WRITING

TIPS, TOOLS, AND TEMPLATES TO WRITE WINNING GRANTS

HOLLY RUSTICK

ISBN: 978-0-9989820-5-2 (e-book)

ISBN: 978-0-9989820-6-9 (print book)

Discover other titles by Holly Rustick at http://www.grantwritingandfunding.com.

For all those dreamers who will turn your dreams into reality.
The world needs you. Keep dreaming, and, more importantly, keep doing.

For all those dreamers who will turn your dreams into reality.
The world needs you. Keep dreaming, and, more importantly, keep doing.

TABLE OF CONTENTS

PREAMBLE

This book is a revised and expanded version of the Amazon Bestseller *Wish Granted! Tips, Tools, & Templates to Write a Winning Grant*.

This book has been revised from the 2017 published book you see pictured above. Why? Well, the information in the previous book still applies, but businesses do grow and change. Since 2017, the book has had a wonderful life, getting in the spotlight several times as a bestseller in various Amazon categories; being required reading for a university; and, most importantly, serving as a guide to help others to write grants and secure hundreds of thousands of dollars (maybe millions by now) for their nonprofits. Yay! This system works!

So, why rock the boat? Well, much of this change is cosmetic. In 2019, I developed new branding for the company and have transitioned the brand, the name of the book, the logos, and the feel to match. I also give away MAD templates in this book, and the URLs have also shifted to match the new branding. Not all of it is just a facelift, though; I have also streamlined my own formula in this book, included updated grant information (as of 2019), and revised the accompanying free mini-course. But beyond that, I have also listened to hundreds of people and their responses to the first book and additional questions. Some questions came up repeatedly, and I have listed some of these questions in this book.

This book may be revised again in the future, but, just as with this edition, the same core principles will remain because, frankly, they work. Why reinvent the wheel when it rolls? You'll see in this book, the wheel is there; it may be similar to other grant books out there because the wheel is the wheel, and they all have similar principles because grant writing is a method. However, where most other grant-writing materials out there are muddied with academic-speak, I use simple language—the kind that would help a single mother with a kid on her hip change a tire on the side of the road. Yep, I explain things straightforwardly, give you templates, and provide an easy-to-remember formula so you can actually use this book. Plus, if you have any questions along the way, you can give me a holler at holly@grantwritingandfunding.com. Enjoy!

WHO THIS BOOK IS FOR

This book is definitely for you if

- You immediately space out and feel your heartbeat quicken when your boss mentions the word "grant"
- You have been tempted to throw your computer against the wall when writing a grant
- You think there are thousands of grants out there for squirrel acrobatics and all your eccentric ideas will get funding
- You had the added role of grant writer or manager dumped in your lap and need some direction and fast-tracked skills
- You are a grant writer but want some additional tips, guidance, or direction
- Your organization receives grants, but maybe not like they used to, and they aren't as competitive
- You want to be a freelance grant writer but need a good resource to refer to as you juggle your clients

What you will learn from this book:

1. the myths and truths of grants
2. different types of grants
3. how to think about grants
4. the G.R.A.N.T.S. formula to fast-track your grant writing
5. how to write a grant narrative
6. how to construct a compelling nonprofit story
7. resources and bonus templates!

What?! All of that? Yes. All of that and more. Keep on reading.

A quick disclaimer: I cannot guarantee that you will secure money overnight by using this book. (Hey, it might happen, but I gotta cover my tush here, too.) However, I am confident that

a. you will increase your knowledge tremendously,

b. the grant-writing process will become a lot clearer, and

c. you will increase your ABILITY to receive funding.

If, and when, you do get funding because you are clearer on grant writing *due to actually reading and completing the exercises in this book or using the templates*, then send me an email! I LOVE it when people receive money for their organization or business after implementing these tips, tools, and templates. Yes, this has happened and more than once or twice.

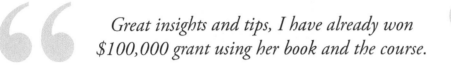

> *Great insights and tips, I have already won $100,000 grant using her book and the course.*
>
> ~ Amazon Customer

As an added benefit, I've put together a free webinar on my website to accompany this book. Some people learn better visually or aurally, so please visit www.grantwritingandfunding.com/bookbonus to sign up for this short webinar as well as for **ALL of the accompanying, downloadable templates**.

If you really want to **elevate your nonprofit and grant-writing skills** and want training, advice, and support to plan, create, and grow profitable and sustainable funding for nonprofits or as a freelance grant writer, then check out the online grant writing course at www.grantwritingandfunding.com/courses.

For ongoing grant updates, resources, and tips, check out my podcast, Grant Writing & Funding, on iTunes, Spotify, or your favorite podcast streaming platform.

HOLLY'S STORY

Hi, Changemaker! My name is Holly Rustick, and I've been on all sides of the coin concerning grants. But how did I get there? Let's rewind to 2005…

Humidity caused the long-sleeved cotton shirt to stick to my back as I leaned forward to get a better look at the sketch on the napkin that Noor held up. It was a little difficult to see as she swung it around in desperation while animatedly speaking in the universal Indonesian language, Bahasa Indonesian.

Once she got a breath in, I looked at her evenly and nodded my head firmly. "Ya, Saya bantu," I said in broken Indonesian and then reaffirmed in English, "Yes, I will help."

Noor was my martial arts instructor. She taught pencak silat *in a dirt lot next to her home. I was learning this sport with a colleague from Australia, Cameron, who was the male sports teacher hired to work at the nongovernment organization (NGO) in Indonesia.*

Not more than six months prior, we would never have been in this province of Indonesia, Aceh, as it had been closed to foreigners for more than 50 years. But a tragedy had changed that in a matter of seconds—a tragedy that had been felt around the world. The earthquake of 2004 had hit the day after Christmas or what people in these parts call Boxing Day. It triggered the largest tsunami ever recorded, which hit dozens of countries and killed a confirmed 184,167 people, displacing more than a million. The province of Aceh (in Northern Sumatra in Indonesia) was the worst hit; it was where 71% of all deaths occurred.

I had been teaching at an all-girls school in Kuwait when this catastrophe happened. I was following the recovery work closely when I saw a job posted online to teach sports for girls for an NGO in Aceh. I promptly applied and, after a phone interview, got the job. As soon as the school year ended, I went to Indonesia to help with community development and to develop programs for the displaced youth.

When I arrived in Indonesia, I realized there was a big problem. The executive director (who was a foreigner) had never done a needs assessment or even asked the community if an afterschool program was what they wanted or needed. After a couple of months, it became apparent that there were larger needs in the community than just teaching sports to youth. Sure, there is a place for sports, but they already had their own sports teachers, and they were now losing out on their pay because of the foreign program. The parents needed jobs, and they needed seed monies to get their businesses re-established so they could better provide for their children.

So, I switched roles and became a student myself, aiming to understand how I could really help. After several months of learning the language; growing relationships with people; and practicing their sport, pencak silat, *I finally got somewhere. After several months, Cameron and I both received our white belts in* pencak silat *along with a trove of five-year-olds. Apparently, this step was also vital to gaining trust, and, eventually, the* pencak silat *instructor, Noor, told me what was really needed. It wasn't foreign sports or largescale infrastructure projects that they had never tried before. It was simple. It was start-up capital to rebuild the industries that once helped the locals lead abundant lives. She personally needed $500 to re-open her water kiosk. All of her supplies had been wiped away in the tsunami, and, though she did make some money teaching* pencak silat, *it wasn't enough to fund the capital investment.*

Noor knew there were some grants available from United Nations agencies but had no idea how to connect with them or how to write a grant or read English. Something clicked at that moment for me. I could do this for her…and for many other people like Noor. What they needed was money for projects that already worked. But they needed a liaison and someone with technical experience to get the money for them. So, I wrote the grant, and I contacted the school in Kuwait I used to work for to do a fundraiser. Noor got money for her kiosk. She also received enough money to go to Jakarta and compete nationally. For only $500, someone's livelihood was recovered, and a dream was attained; a real need was met. This is when I decided to become a grant writer—when I connected mission with money.

I tell you this story so you can really see what motivated me towards grant writing but also to introduce you to many things that this true story represents. We will touch on these throughout this book. You may be curious about what happened to the thousands of dollars it cost to build the wooden school buildings for the sports and other "foreigner" programs. The nonprofit ended up giving the buildings to the community to use as they saw fit. In the process, the village started their own nonprofit with their own mission and vision statement to implement projects that they designed. I returned a few years later, and they still had their nonprofit, but the wooden structure of the school was rotting away. They never used it because they never needed it. In the Needs & Target Demographic section of this book, I'll show you how to ensure that you never make this mistake or that you steer your clients away from making the mistake of creating something they *think* fits a need but actually does not.

So, back to money (because money is fun!).

As you will read in this book, money is a resource. It is nothing to be afraid of or to hoard. It is a method of making your mission happen for your nonprofit or the nonprofits you work with. As a grant writer, you will be a liaison to that money and also a technician. You don't have to go to Indonesia to discover your epiphany of wanting to become a grant writer, but I bet the journey is similar…without traveling halfway around the world. (Although, if you can, it is beautiful, and the people are amazing!)

- You may be really passionate about a certain cause, and you want to help.
- You may have just been tasked to be a grant writer on top of your other roles.
- You may be an executive director or serve on the board of directors of a nonprofit and know the nonprofit needs funding, so you are now in the position of being a grant writer.
- You may be someone who wants to work from home and likes to write.
- You may realize that there is money out there and there are not enough liaisons.

All, or any, of the above reasons are absolutely amazing. Getting grants is wonderful and can have the amazing result of changing one person's life or of improving the lives of thousands of people. In fact, when you are securing hundreds, thousands, or millions of dollars for organizations, the impact of your time and skill is limitless.

I had never really thought of the reach until I was teaching a grant-writing workshop. One of the attendees introduced himself. He stroked his chin thoughtfully and then said, "I have a job right now and can take care of my kids because I am paid from the grant that Holly wrote."

To say I was blown away and humbled by what he said is an understatement. Even though you may be writing grants for projects, you often need to write people into the grant to manage those projects. It really is cool seeing the effect of the impact of the projects, but don't forget the direct affect you will also have to provide for people's livelihoods.

Since that hot and humid day in 2005, I've been writing and securing grants all over the world as well as managing and reviewing grants. I conduct various grant-training workshops and develop products and templates for organizations. I've worked as a technical writer for federal contract bids, facilitated a vast number of fundraising events (from art exhibits to large, high-end galas—I even brought international celebrity Vanessa Williams to Guam!), managed crowd-funding campaigns, and solicited in-kind donations from corporations. I have been a part of any way you can think of getting or giving funding for nonprofits.

If you want to get nerdy, I have a master's degree in International Political Economy that I received while living in Europe. My bachelor's degree, which I received from the University of Hawaii, is in Political Science. I have been published in the academic, fiction, and non-fiction arenas and was the recipient of a resolution from the Guam legislature! (How cool is that?!) I am also a professor at the University of Guam.

In the area of grants, I have been a freelancer and an employee, and I currently own a grant-writing company. Yes, I'm a bit of a geek who tries to remain "cool" while living in awesome places. I've never had the traditional life, and I am happy about that. With the ability to continually think outside the box, I can listen to any challenge that a nonprofit or business faces and immediately come up with a plan for them to make money. To add to my repertoire, I have also taken advanced grant courses and received a slew of grant certificates. Last, but not least, I have written hundreds of grants and have secured millions of dollars for organizations all around the world, helped other grant writers secure funding, and facilitated others to set up and grow freelance grant writing and nonprofit consultant business.

Of course, you don't need a flashy or international resume to be a grant writer and to secure funding. What you do need is a bit of a plan, direction, some tips, and tools. Let's face it: templates don't hurt, and they'll save you hundreds of hours of time and research. I'm here to hold your hand, show you the way, and give you a trove of tools to increase your funding potential for your organization or business.

Are you ready to get started?

SECTION 1:
UNLOCKING THE KNOWLEDGE

CHAPTER ONE

HOW TO USE THIS BOOK

Grants have gotten the rep of being extremely technical and tremendously difficult to write. I'm not going to lie; in some cases, that is true. But…if you have the tools, tips, and templates in this book, you will have a much easier time writing even the most cumbersome of grants. In this short chapter, we will discuss how to use this book to have the most beneficial experience and actually *learn how to write a grant*. That is why you got this book in the first place, right?

This book is designed to help reduce your level of stress associated with writing a grant, diminish or eliminate the more technical parts, and make grant writing a whole lot easier. Like 10× easier. With that being said, probably the most frustrating part of grants is that there are many rules and exceptions to those rules.

It's kind of like the English language. You might not remember learning how to read, but have you ever taught someone how to read (like if you have a five-year-old, this is a perfect example)? Let's just say it like it is: phonetics don't always work.

You hear your five-year-old sounding out a word, and you say, "Actually, that word sounds like this."

Then, the kid asks, "Why?"

You respond, "Er, hmmm, just cuz."

I mean, just take the words "tomb," and "comb"—like, why do those have different "o" sounds? Okay, don't get me started. Grants are not the deep rabbit hole of the English language, but, like English, grants do have many exceptions. So, that's something to keep in mind—but we're not going to get too much into that. Instead, rather than adding another hundred pages trying to explain grant concepts akin to "tomb" versus "comb" so you end up throwing the book against the wall and deciding grants really are too technical and too difficult to write, this book is going to look at more common grants that you will have a **higher likelihood of winning**. We are going to break it down so you will actually USE this book.

I want this book <u>underlined</u>, highlighted, marked up, scuffed up, and located in an easy-to-reach place on your desk.

Your information is going to be written in this book, and it probably won't be something that you will lend to others as some of the information will be specific to your organization. Sure, it can be a great book for your board members, but I wouldn't recommend lending this book out. Feel free to promote it all you want (please do!), but this book should really be purchased for individual or organizational usage. For example, there is a place to enter certain legal numbers, and it also holds all your dreams and goals that won't make sense to someone else who is running a completely different nonprofit or business.

Why write it down? The power of writing things down is amazing.

> *"If you have a goal, write it down.*
> *If you do not write it down,*
> *you do not have a goal—you have a wish."*
>
> ~ STEVE MARABOLI

Writing things down lets you retain and implement what you learn. So, this book is designed as a workbook to help you actually use this information to be a better grant writer as you learn the basics. If you use this workbook, then you will exponentially increase your learning curve on grant writing.

I believe this is so important that I have included this section as a chapter—not a preamble that you skip over. Write in this book! Get out your Post-it notes, grab your highlighters, and do whatever else you need to. If you purchased this as an e-book, then make sure you grab a notebook and write on the cover in permanent marker, "My Grant Writing Book Companion"; you can write the exercises in that.

Watch out for the *tips*, *tools*, and referenced *templates*. Even though you are writing in this book, I have included additional templates and links to the electronic templates so you can use them again and again. You're welcome.

CHAPTER TWO

ABOUT MONEY

"It was the best of times, it was the worst of times, it was the age of wisdom, it was the age of foolishness, it was the epoch of belief, it was the epoch of incredulity, it was the season of light, it was the season of darkness, it was the spring of hope, it was the winter of despair."

~ CHARLES DICKENS

Grant writing is not dead. Sure, it may be taking a backseat right now with political turmoil and forecasts of reduced incentives for corporations to give to nonprofits, but funding hasn't completely disappeared. This is probably one of the most unpredictable times in history for the future of grants, but, in 10 years, we will probably be saying the same thing. There are cycles of recessions, depressions, and political changes throughout history. Don't panic.

Yes, funding may be more competitive. Yes, there may be budget cuts across federal agencies. Yes, it's possible that there will be fewer tax breaks for foundations to give to nonprofits. I'm not saying it's going to be all peaches and cream, but I am also a believer in opportunities.

"Never in the history of America has there been so great an opportunity for practical dreamers as now exists.... This changed world in which we live is demanding new ideas, new ways of doing things, new leaders, new inventions...."

~ NAPOLEON HILL

Napoleon Hill wrote this in the bestselling book, Think and Grow Rich, at one of the worst financial seasons in history—during the Great Depression. But people still became rich by following his advice and practical exercises, and that book is still one of the most popular personal development books with more than 100 million copies sold worldwide.

In this chapter, we are going to do some short money activities. Why? It may have something to do with grants being, er, funding. Money is one of those things in the world that is abstract. Wallace D. Wattles, referring to the riches that can be developed from the ether of thought, wrote, "No one is kept in poverty by shortness in the supply of riches; there is more than enough for all." For our purposes, this book will not go into depth about the law of attraction, but it is important to note the author's philosophy—or physics—on the abundance of money, even if money appears to be hard to get at times.

"Everything is energy, and that's all there is to it. Match the frequency of the reality you want, and you cannot help but get that reality. It can be no other way. This is not philosophy. This is physics."

~ ALBERT EINSTEIN

This book, then, is about how to secure funding. Is it relevant? Yes. Is there still funding available? Yes. Sure, there is funding out there. If federal budget cuts occur, that money will be transferred to other areas. It hasn't disappeared. There are still extremely wealthy people out there; start-up companies will turn into mega-corporations, and newfound actors and athletes will still sign multi-million contracts. Sure, you may have to diversify funding strategies, but you can obtain funding if that is what you want to do and if you follow the system outlined in this book.

"Money grows on the trees of persistence."

~ JAPANESE PROVERB

We will look at other strategies throughout the book, but first, I wanted to take a minute in this chapter to really look at some "freaking out" points. Besides, we are going to be spending time discussing one of the most heated and emotional topics: money. By writing down your challenges (fears) and identifying some solutions, we can be real and get into this book.

"Make your vision so clear that your fears become irrelevant."

~ ANONYMOUS

Are you freaking out about the economy? (Check one):

Yes _____ No _____ Maybe _____

Rewrite this phrase: "Money grows on the trees of persistence."

_____

_____

_____

_____

_____

What is the worst thing that could happen to your organization right now if it lost its funding?

_____

_____

_____

_____

_____

_____

_____

_____

_____

_____

_____

_____

_____

_____

_____

Somehow, when you write your fears down, they tend to lose some of their power. Now that you've got your worries **written down**, and they aren't floating around as a looming monster in your mind, we can move on.

What are some funding strategies that you could immediately set in place to get your organization or business back on its feet if you lost your funding? (*Tip: fundraisers, donations, events, or grants*)

_____

_____

_____

_____

_____

_____

_____

_____

_____

_____

_____

_____

_____

_____

_____

_____

_____

Rewrite this phrase again: "Money grows on the trees of persistence."

_____

_____

_____

_____

_____

If you didn't identify any solutions and instead screamed, "I have no idea what we do!"—that is alright, too. This book is designed to take away a lot of that anxiety and give you the tips, tools, and templates to develop and implement a strategy. We will return to these questions later.

CHAPTER THREE

MYTHS AND TRUTHS OF GRANTS

As a grant writer, I hear a lot of assumptions about grants. The idea that money is just floating around for organizations to grab is real. (It's ironic that most of the people that assume this also are not clear on what they want the money for.)

There are a lot of myths out there about grants *and* grant writers. We will identify these myths and set them straight with truths in this chapter.

Let's start out with a quick little quiz to see where your beliefs are concerning grants. No judgment here. Well, yes, I may poke a little fun at you, but I must say I held a lot of these misconceptions in my own head before I entered the grant-writing world. So, really, I am kind of laughing at myself as well. It is a bit perplexing where these beliefs originated from, but they exist drifting around in conversations and mindsets.

Go ahead and identify where you are by circling your answers below.

1. There are thousands of grants out there for any project or organization.

a. Yes. Like taking candy from a baby

b. No way. Have you seen the budget cuts?

c. There may be lots of grants for specific projects, but that doesn't necessarily mean mine.

2. Grants are free money, and you can do whatever you want with them.

a. Heck, yeah!

b. Nope, you have to pay them back

c. Grants come with strings attached

3. Grants are super easy to get.

a. Yep. Cake.

b. No, you must struggle for weeks over all grants. That's why there are grant writers.

c. Grants are very competitive, and many take a team to write.

4. I might as well just get a grant to pay off my student loan or car debt.

a. Yes, great idea!

b. You can only pay a percentage of it.

c. Hahahaha!

How many As? _____

How many Bs? _____

How many Cs? _____

And no worries on your answers. I will break them all down in the following sections.

To give you a little example, let's look at a guy named Henry. Although Henry is fictional, he is an amalgamation of many real people I have met. Henry thinks that there *must* be **millions of dollars** out there for community organizations that serve those in need. He wants to start a nonprofit organization with a mission to "serve those in need."

Henry thinks that, as soon as the organization is incorporated, money will come out of the woodwork. Henry also thinks that this will happen in two months at the most, at which point he can quit his current full-time job and work for the new nonprofit, receiving the same benefits and salary that he is currently getting—or even at a higher rate. I mean, he can make up his own salary, right? Hmmm...

Let's just start by looking at Henry's mission statement: **"To serve those in need."** That is a pretty broad goal. What kind of needs?

There are many people that have many needs, such as homeless people, victims of crime, single mothers, at-risk youth, those who have fallen behind on mortgage payments, and so on. There are so many needs. Isn't it better to keep your goals broad so you can get more money? Not really.

Think about it. Successful business advertising campaigns are not directed at anyone and everyone. Have you ever noticed that smart companies advertise to very precise populations? Entrepreneurs and marketers talk about creating avatars for the very reason of narrowing your message to a demographic.

It's the same with nonprofit organizations. I mean, let's face it: a lot of times, you need to think of your organization the same way as a **for-profit** organization. Narrowing your mission statement, while keeping it open for various demographics, is important.

What if Henry identified serving the homeless? That is a little bit better. Within his own projects, he would need to think about what kind of homeless individuals he serves.

- Homeless children?
- Veterans who are homeless?
- Domestic violence survivors who are homeless?

The list goes on and on and becomes more and more specific. The mission statement helps the overall framework for the development of projects, but it is important to make your projects increasingly precise. Why? Well, think about if one of the projects was a homeless shelter. When looking at federal guidelines, there are different standards for the square footage required for children, different genders, etc. These are all things to keep in mind when writing your grant.

Does your organization or business have a mission statement? (Check one)

Yes ___ No ___ Not Sure ___

What is your mission statement?

_____

_____

_____

_____

_____

_____

_____

_____

Based on the example above, is it specific enough? (Check one)

Yes ___ No ___ Not Sure ___

Now, let's look at Henry's other idea. He thinks it will only take two months to be up and running as a nonprofit. This may be true, but generally, it takes *much longer* to get all your ducks in a row and for the IRS to review your application and incorporate your organization.

Furthermore, to be up and running with an income that offers hefty wages and benefits in such a short period is a lofty goal. Also, he can't just make up his salary. His salary needs to be justified by what others in his area with similar qualifications earn (refer to the budget chapter for more information regarding this and how to find salaries and wages).

Concerning grant writing, one assumption I hear frequently is that grant writers get paid (pro bono) on commission—i.e., only if the grant gets awarded. You may be one of those people who was asked to write a grant and get paid commission, and that is why you bought this book. This is a big no-no.

We will go over this in more detail in this chapter as it is one that needs further explanation. We will also go over three other false ideas that I often hear from people who usually aren't very familiar with grants. It is an important step to dispel these false beliefs so that you can go forward in knowing the reality about grants as you enter the grant-writing world.

THE MYTHS OF GRANTS

Myth: /miTH/: A widely held but false idea or belief

1. There are thousands of grants available for what you specifically want to do.
2. Grants are "free" money.
3. Grants are super easy to get.
4. Grant writers can just take a percentage of awarded grants to get paid (the commission approach).

These are all common assumptions I hear about grants or grant writers that are false *for the most part*. Why is the grant-writing sector saturated by these beliefs?

But let's be realistic. Most people aren't meditating for days in front of vision boards with pictures of awarded grants. Maybe they should do that, but most are not. Most people aren't even methodical in their approach to winning grants—but you will have that framework by the time you are done with this book!

> *"A misconception remains a misconception,*
> *even when it is shared by the majority of people."*
>
> ~ LEO TOLSTOY

When we hear about organizations that are winning thousands or millions of dollars via grants, we automatically think there is a lot of money out there and that it's easy to get. I mean, those organizations are getting funded; why can't we?

The thing is, we do not usually hear about the hundreds of organizations that applied for those same monies and did not get funded. Or, for that matter, the number of other grants that the same organization applied for and did not get awarded. We may not even know exactly what type of projects the organization is funding or who is writing their grants.

We don't hear about this because it usually isn't discussed in public. After all, what organization wants to publish all the grants that they applied for and didn't get? No one wants to do that. But as soon as the organization gets a grant, it is all over the Internet, newspaper, and radio. Grant writers start boasting about it. It's everywhere. So, it must be easy, right?

DISPELLING MYTHS: THE TRUTH

It's time to dispel some of these myths so you know what you are really facing. This isn't to deflate your hope of getting funding—far from it. But it is better when you know the real challenges you are facing and how to prepare for those challenges than to shoot a hundred bullets in the opposite direction of the bullseye. That is exactly what many people do who operate under the myths of grants: they shoot the wrong way and then end up disheartened, frustrated and broke.

Let's get cracking on this.

1. **Myth:** There are thousands of grants available for what you specifically want to do.

   Truth: There may be only a handful of grants that fit your project, if that.

This seems to be one of the hardest myths to get over, probably because there are a lot of grants available including, at times, very specific ones you never would have thought of. At the same time, this interesting fact makes finding grants more difficult. Sound confusing? It can be a little bit complex. Let's investigate this concept together so you have a better understanding.

Let's say you have a nonprofit organization that operates a soccer club for disadvantaged youth. This seems like a pretty common nonprofit, and it should be easy to get grants, right? Okay, let's find out. On July 7, 2019, I went on the website for federal grants—http:// www.grants.gov—where federal funds are published (more on this later) and typed in "disadvantaged youth soccer" in the search bar. *(Tip: If you want grants.gov to search for all the words combined, you will need to use quotation marks around all the words. Otherwise, the search will entail any of the words.)* There must be thousands of grants to nonprofits that serve disadvantaged youth through soccer, right? Wrong. Guess how many open grant opportunities were identified?

Zero. Zip. Nada.

Let's broaden this search to only include "youth soccer." Take another guess on how many grant opportunities come up. *Drum roll, please.* Once again, zero. Okay, so let's broaden the search even more and just put "youth" in the search bar. Finally! There are 257 grant opportunities published. But now, we need to find out if these potential grant opportunities relate to what your organization does.

At the head of the list is the grant opportunity, "Summer Youth Crew for Habitat Restoration and Community Engagement," and further down the page, "Disability and Rehabilitation Research Projects (DRRP) Program: Independent Living Transition Services for Youth and Young Adults with Significant Disabilities from Minority Backgrounds." The list goes on and on to include everything from runaway youth to youth workforce programs in Pakistan. Yes, Pakistan. As you can tell, there are grants available for very narrow scopes of work. Of course, https://www.grants.gov is not the only place to find grants, but it is a main hub to find <u>federal</u> grants.

Your turn. Go to https://www.grants.gov and type in a word that relates to what you are looking to fund.

Did the word return results? If yes, write down the word or words here:

_____

_____

_____

_____

_____

_____

_____

_____

If not, think of other words and try them out. Once you have some results returned, write down some of the names of grants that you find:

_____

_____

_____

_____

_____

_____

_____

_____

Did these grant opportunities seem to be in line with the projects for which you need funding? (Check one)

Yes _____ No _____ Maybe _____

2. **Myth:** Grants are "free" money.
   Truth: Grants are NOT free money; there is an exchange.

Can't I just get a grant to pursue my master's degree and pay off all my student loans?

Er, no. Another one I hear a lot is, *As soon as we get the grant, we can just use it for whatever we want.* Umm…I'm going to say no again.

Grants are not just free money to use on whatever floats your fancy. Sure, you don't have to pay back grants (unless they are mismanaged, in which case you may have to pay them back), but many grants *are* reimbursable. This means you will have to give receipts to even get monies approved. If you are not submitting receipts for items that were approved in your budget—and for the amount that was approved—you can kiss your reimbursable money goodbye.

Furthermore, funding sources don't sit around asking one another how they can blow through their money. Can you imagine the president of a board of directors for a foundation saying, "Let's go ahead and pay off people's school loans who don't know how to manage their own money"? Yeah, me neither.

Funding sources have purposes and priorities to allocate their money, and—in the case of federal funds—there is legislation to back up the allocation of monies.

When you get that coveted grant awarded, don't throw your proposal out the window and go shopping for a new wardrobe at Versace. You must stick to the budget that you have devised *and* which was approved.

When you have a larger grant, like hundreds of thousands of dollars or millions with many budget line items, then it is unrealistic to think you will follow your budget 100 percent. That is fine, and that is also why there are usually contingencies required to be spelled out in grant proposals (refer to Chapter Eleven). Modifying budgets is also something you normally do *with the permission* and *approval* of your funding source.

Grants are really viewed as an exchange. A funding source has identified priorities that they would like to allocate their money towards, and you, the grantee, step in and raise your hand, saying that you can take their money (i.e., mechanism) and apply it to your project and, thus, fulfill their vision.

3. **Myth:** Grants are super easy to get.
   Truth: Grants are extremely competitive.

The assumption of grants being super easy to get is somewhere up there with grants being super easy to find.

Let's first look at federal grants: We will use www.grants.gov as an example once again to showcase the reality of how difficult it can be to secure grant funding. If we go to one of the first grant opportunities identified in my search for "youth," "Disability and Rehabilitation Research Projects (DRRP) Program: Independent Living Transition Services for Youth and Young Adults with Significant Disabilities from Minority Backgrounds," we see that there are 11 grants of up to $475,000 each, which are available for competition amongst organizations across the entire nation. That's pretty steep competition; there are definitely more than 11 communities in the entire nation that could compete for this grant.

When we look at another grant opportunity, "Summer Youth Crew for Habitat Restoration and Community Engagement," we see that there is only one grant for $52,500. After looking more into this grant, we see that this is specifically for youth in Cuyahoga Valley National Park. So, if you don't live anywhere near this specific National Park and have a youth program, you are not going to be eligible to apply.

By the way, these are all real-time grants at the time of this writing and were in no way referred to me by any sources as they are purely examples. But, hey, if they match what you want to do and are still open when you read this book, by all means, go ahead and apply!

Another place to look is at the number of proposals funding sources receive when they publish a grant opportunity. One of the funding sources that I write a lot of grants for is the Administration for Native Americans Social and Economic Development Strategies.

Tip: This is an awesome grant, so if you meet the priorities of increasing the social and economic development of

Native Americans (including certain Pacific Islanders), you might want to look into it. Once again, they are not sending me any information to publish their name, but I do love this grant.

On average, there may be seven available grants for up to $300,000 per year from this organization. They receive, on average, more than 300 proposals each year for this grant opportunity. That is competitive to say the least. Not only is it competitive when looking at the sheer number of applications, but it is also referred to by some in the industry as one of the hardest federal grants to write. You must have a very well-developed proposal to compete at the higher end, which means you must score around 93 points out of 100 to even be considered for funding. And those points are not so easy to get.

When applying to foundations for funding, it can also be extremely competitive. Getting grants awarded may be a disadvantage for many organizations. What?! For reals.

Listen to this example. A foundation I know got an enormous amount of interest for their 2017 grant cycle request for proposals (RFP). After closing the grant application and realizing the sheer number of applications, the funding source had to decide between only awarding the number of grants they anticipated (i.e., five grants at $10,000 each) or lowering the funding amount and spreading the "wealth" among more organizations (25 grants at $2,000 each). For that year, they chose the latter, which caused the nonprofits to only be able to partially fund their projects. For the foundation, it looked generous because they spread money around their community more. However, in the eyes of each nonprofit, it was ineffective.

Going from writing a grant with a budget of $10,000 to all of a sudden only having $2,000 to spend on the project now caused some of the projects to disappear. One nonprofit had put together a summer camp for their application but, after only receiving $2,000, was only able to purchase a computer and a couple of supplies. How are they going to run a summer camp on a computer? In the end, they were not able to run their project through the grant. Of course, some money can be better than none, but not always. If you are still accountable for completing your objectives but don't have the budget to do it, then you'd better get out there and apply for some matching grants or do some fundraising or crowdfunding.

This just goes to show that there is competition out there, and it is severe at times. Sometimes, you may luck out and be one of the few organizations that have requested a grant and are qualified to run the project, so you get the award. Woo-hoo! That is awesome—but don't think it will always be that way.

Other times, you may get the grant awarded, but when you start the implementation process, you realize it is much more work than you had realized and is taking you away from the mission and vision of your organization. I have seen awarded grants ruin organizations since they were chasing money and applying for shiny pennies instead of focusing on their priorities. Don't be one of these organizations.

Has your organization ever received a grant and then not been able to implement it properly? (Check one)

Yes ____ No_____ Not Sure _____

If yes, what do you think could have been done differently so that this wouldn't have happened?

_____

_____

_____

_____

_____

4. **Myth:** Grant writers can just take a percentage of awarded grants to get paid (the commission approach).

   Truth: In most cases, grants do not include any pre-grant funding to include grant writers. Occasionally, you can write a grant writer into a budget category as a consultant, but only for work they may perform after the grant is funded.

I refer to the commission approach as the unicorn in the sky. Contingency pay is considered an unethical practice and is prohibited by leading professional groups, including the Association for Fundraising Professionals (AFP) and the Grant Professionals Association (GPA). It is very rare that any grant-maker will provide funding eligibility for any pre-award grant work completed, including federal funding sources. If you ignore their rules and go ahead and pay the grant writer, it could even result in the termination of funding.

Besides that, the grant writer has created a product for the organization. They have curated resources and statistics, possibly conducted surveys, held meetings, gathered letters of support, and more to create a product that may be used for future grant applications. Even if the future grant application is for a different project, much of the information that has been created and filed in one document may be used for other grants. The grant product can also help direct an organization's vision, mission, and budget to help guide other fundraising initiatives, such as crowdfunding, fundraising, or getting loans. Even though the actual grant may not be awarded, this product can be utilized for a slew of other funding initiatives.

Excerpt from Podcast & Blog on
www.grantwritingandfunding.com/72
4 ways to utilize the grant as a product:

1. **Update & Resubmit the grant application!** If the grant is not awarded, then ask the funding source that you applied to for feedback.

2. **Update/tweak the grant, and submit it to other open grant solicitations!** You obviously still need money for that project, so find other good-fit funding sources to submit to.

3. **Repurpose the grant application for other funding streams.** You have created a product, and, if it is a good grant application, it has updated statistics to lend credibility to your project, a defined target population, a specific goal, S.M.A.R.T. objectives, a timeline, an evaluation process, a data gathering process, and updated information about your organization.

4. **Provides Clarity.** Just the nature of creating a grant application creates clarity.

No award? Well, the grant writer's name isn't Merlin.

Grant writers are not wizards. They may be very amazing writers, but they are not in control of all factors. Honestly, some funding sources won't even fund an organization until they see your grant application a few years in a row. They want to know that you have staying power. The other thing is that your organization may just not be organized enough. According to Puget Sound Grant Writers Association,

"Proposals succeed or fail for a number of reasons, most of which are out of the grant writer's control. Among these are:

- ✓ **The strength of the project:** The project's feasibility, whether it meets a clear community need, and whether it has a well-planned and realistic budget.
- ✓ **Priorities:** How well the project fits the funder's interests and priorities.
- ✓ **Reputation:** The nonprofit's reputation, track record, and financial history.
- ✓ **Relationships:** How well the funder knows and trusts the nonprofit's board and staff (foundation grants).
- ✓ **Competition:** How many other requests the funder has received and from whom.
- ✓ **Funds and Timing:** How much money the funder has available in this cycle.
- ✓ **Knowledge:** How well the grant writer knows the Funding Opportunity Announcement (FOA), has written or reviewed this grant, and stays up to date on funding changes associated with the grant." (This is really when it comes down to the grant writer in many ways. It's also why I recommend some grant writers to 'niche' down into working with certain grants or types of nonprofits.)

Okay, that's all well and good, but how do you get paid or, if you're a nonprofit, pay your writer?

As a grant writer, it is important that you charge for your services on a non-commission basis. Grant writers will usually charge their clients hourly, by grant application, or on retainer. A grant writer may even look at the total cost of the grant amount that the organization is applying for and charge a percentage flat rate on a non-commission basis. If the organization is applying for a $300,000 grant, they may charge a flat fee of 2% (i.e., $6,000) to be paid whether the grant is funded or not.

Hiring a grant writer is all about an investment in increasing an organization's funding and capacity. A grant writer who does a good job will elevate the organizational structure of an organization in a well-rounded manner. This includes analyzing your board of directors' structure, refining your financial policies and procedures, increasing partners, clarifying your mission and vision, and updating statistics about your target demographic. On top of all that, they will help you get into a good place to get funded.

So, how do you pay a grant writer? Just like you would pay any contractor or consultant. This is an important role, and, just like contracting out any other activity, you can pay the grant writer with those funds. You can also pay the grant writer with money from fundraising or any for-profit arm of your organization that you may have, such as a thrift store or childcare center. If the money is not earmarked for any other purpose, you can utilize this funding to pay the grant writer and increase your capacity.

Excerpt from Podcast & Blog on
www.grantwritingandfunding.com/72
3 Ways a Nonprofit Can Pay a Grant Writer

1. **Fundraise!** The nonprofit can do some fundraising (car washes, bake sales, online fundraiser, etc.) to generate general funds to pay a grant writer!

2. **Generate income from a product or service:** Many nonprofits have thrift stores and cafes, provide counseling, etc. to generate general operating funds for their nonprofit. Having a diversity of income is fundamental for creating healthy nonprofits!

3. **Utilize the Indirect-Cost Rate:** If you utilize an indirect cost rate for your budgets, then including a sustainability developer (or something of that nature) may be something to consider! Refer to this podcast on indirect cost rate for more information!

MYTHS AND TRUTHS OF GRANTS

Now that we have sufficiently beat the myths and truths of grants over the head, let's go ahead and retake that test.

Circle your best answer:

1. There are thousands of grants out there for any project or organization.

a. Yes. Like taking candy from a baby

b. No way. Have you seen the budget cuts?

c. There may be lots of grants for specific projects, but that doesn't necessarily mean mine.

2. Grants are free money, and you can do whatever you want with them.

a. Heck, yeah!

b. Nope, you have to pay them back

c. Grants come with strings attached

3. Grants are super easy to get.

a. Yep. Cake.

b. No, you must struggle for weeks over all grants. That's why there are grant writers.

c. Grants are very competitive, and many take a team to write.

4. I might as well just get a grant to pay off my student loan or car debt.

a. Yes, great idea!

b. You can only pay a percentage of it.

c. Hahahaha!

How many As? _____

How many Bs? _____

How many Cs? _____

Are these different outcomes than your first quiz? If so, what did you learn?

_____

_____

_____

_____

_____

_____

_____

_____

_____

_____

_____

_____

_____

_____

_____

_____

_____

_____

_____

_____

_____

_____

_____

_____

_____

_____

_____

_____

_____

_____

_____

_____

_____

_____

THE ANSWERS:

The answers are all Cs. There may be many grants for specific projects, but that doesn't necessarily mean yours. Grants come with strings attached. Grants are very competitive, and many take a team to write. And, finally, you're dreaming if you think a grant will pay off your self-inflicted debt. Yes, that one always makes me laugh. Of course, there are minimal grants out there that might pay for arrears for those who are in extreme poverty, but that is different from any Joe Schmo racking up debt at some random college and then thinking some funder will wave a magic wand and make it disappear so he/she can travel to Asia for a year while using credit cards.

"We live in a culture that quit asking, 'How much?' and instead asks, 'How much down, and how much a month?'"

~ DAVE RAMSEY

In Chapter Three, you learned about the myths and truths of grants. We dispelled myths to discover the truths about grants:

1. There may only be a handful of grants that fit your project—if that.
2. Grants are NOT free money; there is an exchange.
3. Grants are extremely competitive.
4. In most cases, grants do not include any pre-grant funding for grant writers. Occasionally, you can write a grant writer into a budget category as a consultant, but only for work he/she may perform after the grant is funded.

Remembering these truths as you move forward in grant writing will help you stay on track and not get easily discouraged, but you also need to know about another big elephant in the room....

TIPS

✓ Make sure your mission statement is one to two sentences and is clear and memorable. *(Check out https://www.grantwritingandfunding.com/067-values-mission-and-vision for more information and examples!)*

✓ When you're doing grant research on grants.gov and you want to search for a phrase, you will need to use quotation marks around all the words. Otherwise, the search will entail any and all of the words.

✓ The Administration for Native Americans Social and Economic Development Strategies grant is an awesome grant, so—if you meet the priorities of increasing the social and economic development of Native Americans (including certain Pacific Islanders)—then you might want to look into it. Once again, they are not sending me any information to publish their name, but I do love this grant.

TOOLS

✓ For federal grants, visit http://www.grants.gov.

✓ For podcasts and blogs related to mission and vision and how to pay a grant writer, check out www.grantwritingandfunding.com/podcasts.

TEMPLATES

✓ For a grant research template, visit www.grantwritingandfunding.com/bookbonus.

NOTES:

CHAPTER FOUR

THE MINDSET BEHIND GRANTS

Okay, what is a grant? Most of you probably already know what a grant is. But let's get into the nitty gritty for a second.

A grant is money given by an organization, most notably by a government, for a particular purpose.

Here, I would like to stress the words *"for a particular purpose"* because, if you get a grant awarded and then spend the money on something else, you are not acting in good faith and may have to return the money. I want to spend another moment here to really drive this point home. Even though you may think, "Of course! I got this!", you really need to understand this point.

An organization, agency, or person has monies and a vision for those monies. When you apply for these monies, your vision must align with their vision. A great analogy is the parent/teenager relationship when the teenager asks the parent for money.

What is a grant? Rewrite the phrase "A grant is money given by an organization, most notably by a government, for a particular purpose."

_____

_____

_____

_____

_____

_____

_____

TIME WARP

Let's go back into the past…to when you were 15 years old. And, while we are at it, let's change your name to Charlene. You are very athletic and absolutely love your soccer team, but, at times, your grades have dropped because you prioritize your practice over homework. Recently, you were picked for the senior soccer team, and you need some money for a new uniform and for the registration fee. You are going to ask your parents for the $50 uniform and $100 registration fee, but you know you must make a bit of a case to get the money because your grades dropped a lot last soccer season. Nevertheless, you are so stoked because, as a sophomore, you've been chosen for the senior team! So, you start devising a little plan in your mind. You will carve out an hour every night to work on homework and get your grades back up. Okay, good plan. Now, you are confident to approach your parents.

Charlene: "Hi, Mom and Dad! I can't believe it—I was chosen for the senior soccer team!"

Mom: "Wow! Awesome!"

Dad: "Hmm…this will be even more work than last season."

Charlene: "Um, yeah, but it's so exciting…."

Dad: "So, how much are the soccer dues?"

Charlene: "Well, they are around $100 for registration, and I need $50 by tomorrow for the uniform."

Mom: "Well, that's just the start, but you'll also need money for away games and everything else. And, like your dad said, it'll be more work than last season—and that's when your grades dropped."

Charlene: "I'll keep my grades up by setting aside 8 to 9 every evening to do my homework and chores."

Dad: "Okay, that sounds like a good plan."

Mom: "Here's $50. It's already after 8. Why don't you go ahead and get started on your studying?"

Sound like a typical scenario? What I love about this example is that we know even as teenagers (and even younger) how to devise objectives, measures, and reporting. We basically know how to write a grant. The concept is really that simple…of course, with some added research, text, and formatting. Charlene knows that her parents have a priority to support her in the best way, but she also knows that her parents have priorities of academic grades and want to know that she can handle the project (in this case, soccer).

But let's just say something happens the next day. You are out with your new team at McDonald's and are excited to be the youngest soccer player. The coach announces he has extended gathering uniform money for one more day. One of the players sees that you have some money on you and says she left her money at home. To please her, you buy her dinner. Then, you think, "What the heck?" and buy hamburgers all around for everyone. There goes your $50 for your uniform. But then again, you felt cool paying for everyone's hamburgers and got the nickname "money bun."

That night, you go back to your parents.

Charlene: "Hey, Mom and Dad, er, I need another $50 for my soccer uniform."

Dad: "What happened to the $50 your mom gave you last night?"

Charlene: "It's kind of a long story."

Mom: "What?! *Explicit word inserted here.*"

This is what you need to think of in a funding source. They are like a parent. They need receipts. They want reports. They want to know that you are fulfilling your part of the deal. Remember, you can't just ask your parents for anything. If they don't think soccer is a good idea and beneficial to you, they probably won't give you the money for a soccer uniform.

THE MINDSET BEHIND GRANTS

Having a clear understanding of how to think about grants is very important. When you are looking for and writing a grant, keep the metaphor of the teenager/parent relationship in your mind's eye. This is a great idea for when you are formulating your needs, objectives, and evaluation sections.

We will go over each of these sections in later chapters. Before we get there, let's do another activity to make sure you really understand the mindset behind grants.

Can you spend money on whatever you want after you get a grant awarded? (Check one)

Yes ___ No ___ Maybe ___

If you checked "no," you are correct! It is so important to spend money on what you said you were going to spend it on—regardless of whether your soccer team all wants hamburgers. If you need to change any spending, then you may have to ask for a budget modification.

What? Okay, let me explain. Grants may allow for a certain percentage of money to be shifted from one main category to another. *Note: I did not say to newly devise categories but pre-existing approved categories.* If you do want to shift some monies around, the contract should specify what the percentage allowances are that can be made without pre-approval or what percentage requires approval or is not allowed at all. If you are scratching your head, just go ahead and call up your grant officer from the agency that awarded you the grant. For example, a grant may allow you to shift 10% of the entire budget between line items without requiring a formal budget modification. But, once again, this is between line items that have already been approved. In any event, I would still let the grants officer know what you are doing to allow for transparency.

Some grants are so small that they don't allow for many changes at all. Again, keep the teenager/parent relationship scenario in mind. Funding sources want to think the best of you. Just like many teenagers may need to prove that they are trustworthy to their parents, organizations must prove themselves trustworthy to funding sources.

In this chapter, you learned the mindset behind grants. Once you receive a grant, please be sure to remember that your funding sources are akin to your parents, and you are the trustworthy and responsible teenager.

"A relationship without trust is like having a phone with no service. And what do you do with a phone with no service? You play games."

~ANONYMOUS

TIPS

✓ When you are looking for or writing a grant, keep the metaphor of the teenager/parent relationship in your mind's eye).

✓ Only spend your grant monies on eligible expenses in your budget. No hamburgers in place of soccer uniforms, Money Bun.

TOOLS

✓ Common sense! Just pinch yourself if you start spending money without looking at your approved budgets.

TEMPLATES

✓ None.

NOTES:

CHAPTER FIVE

THE DIFFERENT TYPES OF GRANTS

Grants, grants, grants. There are many different types of grants.

This section is generally when people's eyes start to glaze over. I know mine can start to get heavy at this point too, so I will try and keep this section informative, basic, and short.

When I am facilitating grant trainings, this is when I wish I was a ventriloquist and could have my princess dummy explain the different grants in a Kermit the Frog voice. Maybe, just maybe, we could all get through it without glazed eyes. Without the talent of being a ventriloquist or being live in front of you, though, I invite you to use your imagination and read this chapter in an internal Kermit voice.

In this chapter, we will go over the main types of grants: federal grants, state and government grants and contracts, and foundation grants. By the end of the chapter, you should be able to know if your organization is eligible for certain types of grants. You will also be able to understand some very important grant lingo.

Alright, everyone got your Kermit voice on? Let's go…

FEDERAL GRANTS

In the United States, federal grants are economic aid issued by the federal government. These grants are awarded to organizations or individuals to carry out a specific purpose of the United States government.

Types of federal grants:

- Categorical grants: Narrowly defined purposes (i.e., categories). Much of the time, recipients must match a percentage of the grant.

  1. Project grants: Fund research (medical, science, etc.) and other projects
  2. Formula grants: Determined by law

- **Block grants:** Large grants given to state or local governments for a general purpose. The states and territories then disperse these monies: think Medicaid and Temporary Assistance to Needy Families (like food stamps).

- **Earmark grants:** Specified in the appropriations of the U.S. Congress and are not competitive grants. We are not going to talk about this one, but I wanted to include it with the different types in case you come across it.

We are going to concentrate on **categorical project grants** since these are the most competitive for nonprofits and organizations. There are 26 federal grant-making agencies. This is where the money for federal grants originates. To say that federal grants are political is an understatement.

BREAKING IT DOWN

There are more than **900 grant programs** offered by the 26 federal grant-making agencies.

These programs fall into 20 categories:

Agriculture	Disaster Prevention and Relief	Food and Nutrition	Law, Justice and Legal Services
Arts	Education Regional Development	Health	Natural Resources
Business and Commerce	Employment, Labor, and Training	Housing	Science and Technology
Community Development	Energy	Humanities	Social Services and Income Security
Consumer Protection	Environmental Quality	Information and Statistics	Transportation

If you were to go on to any federal agency website right now, you would see that all federal grants fall under one of these categories.

What are some categories that immediately pop in your mind concerning your nonprofit or organization?

_____

_____

_____

_____

_____

_____

---

e.g., If you are part of a nonprofit that has a substance abuse recovery program for pregnant women, then there are a few categories that you might want to investigate: Housing; Health; and Employment, Labor, and Training. Of course, there could be grants within other categories, but this gives you an idea of the umbrellas of funding categories.

REGULAR VS. COOPERATIVE GRANTS

Regular grants

Regular grants are just what they sound like: regular. They are your basic, run-of-the-mill grants that are available. You will need to identify if you and your project are eligible to receive these grants. Ineligibility and eligibility are usually spelled out clearly within the FOA.

Who can apply?

These eligibilities and ineligibilities will outline who can even apply, i.e., nonprofit organizations with IRS tax exemption status, individuals, researchers, and so forth. Sometimes, any or all listed above may also be ineligible to apply for the grant.

What projects can be funded?

FOAs or RFPs will also list eligible and ineligible projects. So, first, find out if your organization or association can even apply for the grant. Then, move on to priorities and see if the project that you want to be funded is eligible. This goes back to the section on **mindset** as your project needs to align with the funding source's priority, vision, and mission.

Put your detective magnifying glass on this section. For instance, you may have operating expenses that need to be covered (When do you NOT?), but that particular grant may state that operating costs are an ineligible expense. Of course, there are always ways to cover operating costs (see budget chapter). Other items, such as vehicles, food, travel, etc. may also be considered ineligible expenses. Make sure you review the ineligibilities and eligibilities before you go on and write a 50-page grant and spend a week putting together a triple A boss budget. It would really be frustrating to formulate your entire project around creating an Uber-like company if you can't allocate funding towards vehicles. Just saying.

Okay, so, back to the regular grant. *Side note: Do you think they could come up with a better word to describe it? I mean it makes like perfect sense in a very boring "yadda, yadda, yadda" way that may put you to zzzzzzz. Oh, too late.* Alright, with *regular* grants there will be reporting requirements, but—compared to cooperative agreements— the federal government is relatively hands-off. Now, "cooperative" is a much better word, although it does remind me of a hippie co-op store that is run by people with dreadlocks eating granola (no offense—I ate a ton of granola in the 90s).

COOPERATIVE AGREEMENTS

When an awarding agency is going to get more involved in the grant process, such as additional routine monitoring and technical assistance, they will implement a cooperative agreement. The level of involvement to mandate a cooperative agreement varies amongst federal agencies and even within programs.

For cooperative agreements, the federal government offers a great deal of hand-holding and many directives, but there are three common items:

1. robust oversight

2. technical assistance

3. webinars, conference calls, site visits, etc.

A cooperative agreement could be a highly specialized research award where the federal staff and recipient will be conducting the research together. I tend to like cooperative agreements as the grantee gets trained in many ways on how to oversee a project and has regular accountability. However, many people do not like them as you are required to get many pre-approvals from the federal government, which may slow down some processes. Even so, I find that those who are new to federal grants can benefit a lot from having a cooperative grant agreement.

MATCHING AND CHALLENGE GRANTS

Matching and challenge grants can be either regular or cooperative grants. Think budget. Matching grants are nonfederal monies that you secure to "match" the federal portion of the grant.

> **Matching:** A nonfederal share of a grant to show community buy-in, which can be either a hard (cash) or soft (in-kind) match.

The organization must show where they will get the **nonfederal** matching funds. The best thing to do is to include a signed and dated letter of commitment from your source for the nonfederal matching value. So, if you are applying for a matching regular grant and must come up with a 20% match, you cannot use another federal grant that you already received for that match. You could use it for leveraged support, but not for matching. This must be **nonfederal** matching, meaning the source of cash or in-kind (when allowed) sources must be *other* than federal funds. This can get a little confusing.

Okay, so, while you are still scratching your head, I'll go ahead and get a little bit geekier for a second. It's important to pay attention to any pass-through federal funds as well. For instance, if you are receiving a contract from the state, some of the funds allocated to the state contract might be from the federal government. Either ask the contracting financial officer from the state contract or grant to give you the breakdown of where the funds are derived from or dig around in the contract and try to find it yourself. Sometimes, this is broken down by percentage.

The state agency may have 50% of the contract funds allocated from the federal government. This is known as a *pass-through* since the federal government is allocating funds for a certain priority—sometimes in the form of a block grant—and then, the state agency awards the monies locally through a formula or discretionary grant. The federal government is literally passing money through the state to award and manage. The remaining 50% could be funded by taxpayers directly from the state and are local grants (nonfederal). I would be hesitant to match these monies to your grant as it is all mixed up in one contract and usually for one scope of work. *Tip: Know what pass-through funds your organization receives. For example, you may receive direct federal grants for*

$650,000 and think you are off the hook for a required audit. But your organization receives $800,000 in federal funds because a contract your organization has with a state agency amounts to $200,000 in federal pass-through funds. Danger, danger! You now must get an audit because you surpassed the amount of $750,000 from federal funds in a given year.

HARD MATCH VS. SOFT MATCH

Hard match = cash

Soft match = in-kind

A *hard* match is when you get cash (nonfederal) to match your grant. This could be actual cash raised through fundraising, donations, program income (say you have a coffee shop, sell products, etc.), or other cash. I'll say it once again. You cannot use money from a federal grant as a federal match—even if it is from another agency—unless, in a very rare case, it clearly specifies that you can. (This is very uncommon, and I have only seen it from the Community Development Block Grant). Call the program officer to verify if you can utilize your federal grant as a match for any other grant, and then have them send you an email with the clause.

In-kind, otherwise known as a *soft* match, is when you use sources and give them a value. A company may be housing your project at a facility at no cost, but you could validate the value of that space. All you would have to do is show the fair market value for that facility—say $1,000 per month—through a letter that the owner is allowing you the space at no cost, which is a $12,000-per-year nonfederal match that can be included in your matching grant. Otherwise, you could show the lease, which identifies the cost and agreement. In either of these ways, you would show that $12,000 per year is an **in-kind** cost.

Obviously, the grant you are applying for would have to use that space exclusively for it to be used as an in-kind source; if you wanted to use the 1,000-square footage facility valued at $1,000 per month for in-kind matching, but your project never utilized the space, then you couldn't use it as a match. The matching and in-kind allocation must be in direct support of the project that you are writing the grant for.

Ideas and examples for in-kind matching

ACTIVITY	TYPE	COMPUTATION	NOTE
Meetings to support the project	Must be nonfederal volunteers	Track their hourly rate, i.e., $22/hr. (volunteer rate) × 1.5 hours × 12 meetings per year × 10 people = $3,960	If the volunteer has a specialized degree, is acting as a CPA for your org, is a traditional healer, etc., you give him/her a different hourly rate that makes sense with his/her experience and what he/she is contributing $22 per hour is just an example.
Volunteers who coordinate training	Must be nonfederal volunteers	Track their hourly rate, i.e., $50/hr. (volunteer rate) × 5 hours × 6 weeks × 2 people = $3,000	If the volunteer has a specialized degree, is acting as a CPA for your org, is a traditional healer, etc., you give him/her a different hourly rate that makes sense with his/her experience and what he/she is contributing. $50 per hour is just an example.
Vehicles to transport beneficiaries	Must not be purchased with federal fund	Track the mileage and maintenance used to drive beneficiaries to approved services.	You can use the federal mileage rate: https://www.irs.gov/uac/2017-standard-mileage-rates-for-business-and-medical-and-moving-announced
Internship students	Must not be getting paid from the project	Track the time of the intern in line with what their level of expertise amounts to.	
Supplies	Could be supplies donated or secured through fundraising	Track the costs of supplies, such as printing, paper, uniforms, etc.	
Rentals	If someone is donating space to you at no cost	Include the lease agreement or letter of commitment with a rental rate that is no more than the fair market standard.	

More information about tracking in-kind matching can be found in Chapter Ten.

Challenge Grant: A challenge grant is normally a hard or cash match. For example, a funding source may request that the nonprofit or individual raise $5,000, and, once the organization has secured that $5,000 (or shows letters of commitment for the money), then the funding organization will give you the $80,000 grant or whatnot. The concept is the funding source wants to see that your project can get other types of support. Many organizations use the purchase of food from an outside source as a challenge grant since food is basically an ineligible cost for so many federal and foundation grants. In my experience, challenge grants are not as pervasive as *matching grants*, so I am not going to go into depth about challenge grants. But this gives you an idea of what they entail.

STATE AND GOVERNMENT GRANTS

Definition

State and local governments often receive much of their funding from the federal government as they can promote economic efficiency due to localized knowledge to implement a program more efficiently and effectively than the federal government (i.e., pass-through funding). These grants may help foster policy experimentation at the state and local levels that would be difficult to achieve in a single national program. Other ways of funding state government grants are via state tax dollars. The amount of funding and percentage of funding for state grants varies from state to state.

FORMULA VS. DISCRETIONARY GRANTS

Formula grant programs are noncompetitive awards based on a predetermined formula. These programs are sometimes referred to as state-administered programs. A formula grant is a type of mandatory grant that is awarded based on statistical criteria for specific types of work. There is an actual formula to allocate costs. Medicaid is an example of a formula grant. Per legislation, there is an open-ended matching formula in which the federal government provides matching funds to state governments for all activities that fall within Medicaid coverage. If regulations are followed, and the services are compliant, the state receives the grant monies.

Additionally, formula grants are generally for U.S. state, local, or territory governments rather than for private organizations. Individuals do not directly receive formula grants.

Discretionary grants are funds awarded through a competitive process. The agency reviews applications, in part through a formal review process and peer-review panel. Discretionary grants are most commonly what you will seek.

Contracts are basically either made through grant formulas or discretionary funding through federal, state, or government agencies. These differ in regular and cooperative grants in the formalities. If we were to compare the two mechanisms, we would say that a contract has two parties exchanging promises where one party delivers and the other party pays. A grant, however, has two parties wherein one party gives the money and another party performs the objectives in hopes of achieving them. A contract is legally binding, and nonperformance can be dealt with in court whereas nonperformance of a grant can result in the organization paying back monies and essentially being blacklisted.

List some examples of state or government grants in your area:

_____

_____

_____

_____

_____

_____

_____

_____

_____

_____

_____

_____

_____

_____

_____

_____

_____

_____

_____

_____

_____

_____

_____

_____

_____

_____

_____

_____

_____

_____

_____

_____

FOUNDATIONS

"A foundation is a non-governmental entity that is established as a nonprofit corporation or a charitable trust with a principal purpose of making grants to unrelated organizations, institutions, or individuals for scientific, educational, cultural, religious, or other charitable purposes."

~ GRANTSPACE

A *foundation grant* is monetary assistance provided to individuals and small businesses by companies, citizens, government, and non-government organizations. The money awarded as a **grant** is meant to meet **particular needs** and is not required to be repaid.

Once again, this isn't free money. Foundation grants are awarded to others who are the best match to carry out the vision and mission of the foundation. The foundation may still ask for reports and receipts. Many times, when you receive grants from foundations, it is from foundations in your community. Therefore, they may be familiar with what your organization does and will know (and see) that your organization is being responsible in implementing the grant. This transparency could be vital in your organization continuing to win awards each time the foundation opens their grant cycle. Many foundations do not even receive unsolicited grants or may not in the future, so it is important that your organization is consistent and persistent in developing a relationship with these foundations.

Tip: Get on the good side of a foundation.

A *private foundation* is a nongovernmental, nonprofit organization having a principal fund managed by its own trustees or directors. Private foundations award monies to charitable, educational, religious, or other activities serving the public good, primarily through the making of grants to other nonprofit organizations. A private foundation usually derives its principal fund from a single source, such as an individual, family, or corporation. A private foundation does not solicit funds from the public.

When you think of private foundations, think the Ford Foundation, the Bill & Melinda Gates Foundation, local insurance companies in your community that have foundations, and the like. I am highlighting some mega-foundations and smaller foundations to show you both the range and the differences in foundations. For example, larger private foundations, such as the Bill and Melinda Gates Foundation and the Ford Foundation, are ones that a lot of people who believe the "myths of grants" refer to before they write a grant. They think that, because these organizations award millions of dollars every year, a piece of that millionaire pie should come directly to them. It could, I will give them that, but it only will if your organization is a perfect match for the funding and beats out the incredible competition.

PUBLIC CHARITIES

Public charities generally derive their funding or support primarily from the general public, receiving grants from individuals, government, and private foundations. Although some public charities engage in grantmaking activities, most conduct direct service or other tax-exempt activities.

When you think of public charities, think of organizations such as your local public radio stations, the Jane Goodall Institute, Goodwill Industries International, and the like. These public charities usually don't publish grant opportunities as they raise money (usually in large part from the public) and contribute directly to their cause.

In a way, public charities are like a hybrid nonprofit organization. If you are an NPR radio listener, you will be familiar with hearing your local radio station asking listeners to donate to run the radio station during their semi-annual telethons. This is a form of public charity.

The Jane Goodall Institute is another example. You have probably heard of Dr. Jane Goodall, an amazing woman who has created awareness and advocacy for wildlife in Africa. The Jane Goodall Institute "promotes understanding and protection of great apes and their habitat and builds on the legacy of Dr. Jane Goodall." The Institute requests monies from individuals, organizations, and other entities primarily through monthly giving and other campaigns.

You have probably also heard of Goodwill stores. The noted mission of Goodwill Industries International is "to enhance the dignity and quality of life of individuals and families by strengthening communities, eliminating barriers to opportunity, and helping people in need reach their full potential through learning and the power of work." By receiving donations (both monetary and in-kind donations such as clothing, furniture, and other items), Goodwill Industries International can fulfill their mission of assisting others. This is another great example of a public charity.

Write out what your priority area is for your organization *(e.g., projects for the blind, homeless shelters for victims of abuse, conservation projects, etc.)*

_____

_____

_____

_____

_____

_____

_____

_____

Write down any current foundations you are aware of in your community.

_____

_____

_____

_____

_____

_____

_____

_____

_____

_____

_____

_____

_____

Look up those foundations and write down what location they fund. If you don't know of any, Google foundations in your city or region, and write down the locations they fund.

_____

_____

_____

_____

_____

_____

_____

_____

_____

_____

_____

_____

_____

_____

_____

_____

Now, look at the priority areas that these foundations fund and write down those that match your organization's priority areas.

_____

_____

_____

_____

_____

_____

_____

_____

_____

_____

_____

_____

_____

_____

_____

DIFFERENT TYPES OF GRANTS

Having knowledge about the different types of grants is important because you are now able to understand what the heck all this lingo means and go after grants that make the most sense for your organization. I get that this section was a lot of information, but the good news is that the more time you spend researching grants, the easier it will be to wrap your brain around all this terminology. Federal and state grants are probably the driest as far as terminology goes, but they are also the most straightforward. Foundation grants can seem more "fun," but they are the ones that have a lot of variances in the way you should apply. Foundation grants can take the most time to research, although, much of the time, they may not request as much information as comprehensive and complex federal grants. There are definitely pros and cons to both.

So, which grants should your organization apply for? The answer is, all that your organization is eligible for and that make sense for your projects. And don't make the mistake of shooting off the same application to all foundations or federal granting agencies. That doesn't make sense, and they will more than likely just throw out your generic proposal.

"The biggest barrier to starting a company isn't ideas, funding, or experiences.
It's excuses."

~ SARAH LACY

In this chapter, you learned what the heck the different types of grants are and which ones are the best for your organization. Here's a quick cheat sheet for all the grant lingo. You can also find a template at www. grantwritingandfunding.com/bookbonus.

FEDERAL GRANTS (THREE MAIN TYPES BELOW)	
CATEGORICAL:	Defined purposes (the one you will most often apply to)
BLOCK GRANTS:	Large grant given to state or local government for a general purpose
EARMARK GRANTS:	Specified monies appropriated by the U.S. Congress; not competitive
FORMULA GRANTS (FEDERAL OR STATE):	Noncompetitive awards based on a predetermined formula
DISCRETIONARY GRANTS:	Funds awarded through a competitive process (federal or state):
REGULAR GRANTS:	Basic grants
COOPERATIVE GRANTS:	When awarding agency is heavily involved in the grant process
MATCHING GRANT:	Nonfederal monies required to match the federal grant. The percentage varies from grant to grant, and not all grants include matching amounts
CHALLENGE GRANT:	A challenge grant is derived from hard match (cash) and is nonfederal
HARD MATCH:	Cash
SOFT MATCH:	In-kind (such as the value of the time of volunteers, the value of rent or of a lease if you are not being charged that cost, etc.)
FOUNDATION GRANT:	Monetary assistance meant to meet particular needs and not required to be repaid
PRIVATE FOUNDATION:	Nongovernmental, nonprofit organization having a principal fund managed by its own trustees or directors
PUBLIC CHARITIES:	Although some public charities engage in grantmaking activities, most conduct direct service or other tax-exempt activities

TIPS

✓ Know which pass-through funds your organization receives. For example, you may receive direct federal grants for $650,000, so you think you are off the hook for a required audit. But your organization receives $800,000 in federal funds because a contract your organization has with a state agency amounts to $200,000 in federal pass-through funds. Danger, danger! You now must get an audit because you surpassed the amount of $750,000 of federal funds in a given year. Get on the good side of a foundation.

TOOLS

✓ For federal mileage rates, visit https://www.ifebp.org/news/regulatoryupdates/Pages/2019-irs-mileage-rates.aspx.

✓ For information about federal grants, visit https://www.grants.gov.

✓ For information on foundations, visit https://www.guidestar.org.

TEMPLATES

✓ For a downloadable cheat sheet on the different types of grants, visit www.grantwritingandfunding.com/bookbonus.

✓ For a downloadable grant research sheet, visit www.grantwritingandfunding.com/bookbonus.

NOTES:

CHAPTER SIX

ORGANIZING THE GRANT TEAM

I have been tasked many times to write grants with absolutely no support. This is not the best way to write a grant. What has happened is that I have written these beautiful and "perfect" grants that have gotten awarded.

Sounds great, right?

The downfall is that, without the input of the team, these grants have not always been implemented in the best way. As a project manager, human resource manager, or whatever position you may hold at your company, I encourage you to pester the heck out of people to support you when writing a grant.

If you are the grant writer at a company or a grant-writing consultant, you still need to bug people. The thing is, everybody is super busy, and that is why they are dumping the grant writing on your lap. I get it.

Very small nonprofit organizations can be the worst at times because most staff are doing above and beyond, are burned out, and may not be compensated adequately. I get this, too. I have worked in a lot of small nonprofits and understand that everybody is tasked to death. But I also know that one of the main ways to reduce burdens and burnout is to get grants awarded to hire additional staff, increase overall salaries, and grow the capacity of the organization. Therefore, most of the staff are dependent on your ability to get grants awarded.

Paradoxically, if staff members are not tasked with grant-writing sections or responsibilities, they may turn and run from you in the hallway or not prioritize responding to your emails. Many times, this is not their fault; it is an ideology woven into the fabric of the organization and is often a result of poor leadership or ignorance about the grant-writing world. This can even go back to the myths of grants wherein leaderships think grants are just so easy to get, so they don't set up the right type of support system for those who are doing the grant writing.

"A goal without a plan is just a wish."

~ ANTOINE DE SAINT-EXUPÉRY

I've said all of this to say, **set up your team**. In this chapter, I will outline…

- ✓ **Grant team members**
- ✓ **A checklist of what needs to be discussed**

Are you ready to have an actual productive meeting?

GRANT TEAM MEMBERS

The ideal grant team comprises the lead grant writer, the budget lead, the grant coordinator, and potential specialists. The executive director should really oversee the process and be involved in the design, but he or she should ultimately be someone to whom you report and who reviews the grant, and it may be the one who submits the grant. We will talk about the process below, but first, let's go ahead and identify the team members.

The **lead grant writer** should be the main writer that pulls together all sections. Yes, you can have different people writing different parts of the grant, but this can lead to a very disjointed grant. When reviewing grants, I can tell when there was or was not a clear lead. This often results in a very poorly scored grant because it is not cohesive.

For example, if the budget lead writes the budget and includes the purchase of two computers and one regional training for two staff members, but then the person writing the project approach never talks about the use of computers or the regional training, this can lead to confusion on the reviewer's part.

To make matters worse, suppose the grant coordinator writes the project design section with a goal of housing for homeless people, but there is no allocation for housing in the budget. Yes, I have seen these inconsistencies in grants. The lead grant writer should get all the information needed but should be the one to actually write the grant to make sure the style is consistent and that all sections fit together cohesively.

The **budget lead** should put together the budget and the nonfederal matching amounts. The budget lead should be able to give the grant lead adequate information and budget computations so that the grant writer can flesh out the budget narrative. The budget lead is usually your fiscal staff.

The **grant coordinator** is the one who can follow up and get additional information. For example, the grant coordinator will send out the letters of commitment and memorandums of understanding and will curate resumes and job descriptions. The grant coordinator will work closely with human resources and project managers to gather all additional information. He or she will also track all letters secured and still outstanding.

A **specialist** may be needed at times to write a particular section of the grant, such as evaluation methodology, evidence-based practices, and so on.

The **executive director** or **board of directors** should be who you report to, and they should be who leads the design of the proposal before you even start to write. They should review the grant and finalize all information. Additionally, they are usually the ones to submit the grant application. At times, they may give the lead grant writer authority to submit grants online, but they should at the very least review the grant in a timely manner so you are not trying to upload the grant at the very last minute. Ultimately, whoever is responsible for submitting the grants (make sure you designate someone; don't assume who will do it!) should make sure your grants.gov password and SAM number are up to date. At times, you (the grant lead) may be fulfilling any and all of these job descriptions.

Fill in below:

Executive Director or Board of Directors

_____

_____

Grant Lead (usually yourself)

_____

_____

Budget Lead (usually fiscal agent/accountant/bookkeeper)

_____

_____

Grant Coordinator

_____

_____

_____

Grant Submission Officer (clarify if this is the executive director, lead grant writer, etc.)

_____

_____

_____

As for the flow of the grant-writing team, you should have an initial meeting after the FOA has already been reviewed.

A CHECKLIST OF WHAT NEEDS TO BE DISCUSSED

Avoid meetings that drone on and on and get nothing accomplished. I created a checklist for you so you can facilitate a meeting and get all the information that you need. In this way, you will gather all the information needed for the grant, and you will be professional and efficient in getting the information.

Visit www.grantwritingandfunding.com/bookbonus to download a grant kick-off meeting checklist and an action plan timeline template to utilize. We will also be looking at the work action timeline in more detail in a later chapter. Ultimately, you will clarify your objectives and goals and then start listing all the activities needed to reach the objectives. Your team should meet weekly (or more frequently closer to the deadline) to report on the status in meeting all deadlines.

Before you even start writing the grant, make sure you have read the FOA or RFP and have a kickoff grant meeting. Identify all leads and responsibilities of key people, and start your action plan timeline. Here is a checklist to go over for your kickoff grant meeting.

1. Is the nonprofit's SAM number up to date?

2. Is the nonprofit registered on grants.gov?

3. Who will submit the grant?

4. What types of letters of support/Memorandums of Understanding/letters of commitment, etc. are required?

5. Who will be tasked with gathering any required letters?

6. When is the deadline for gathering the letters?

7. Are there any matching funds required?

8. If yes, where will the matching funds come from?

9. Who will gather all necessary letters or proof of matching funds?

10. Who will be in charge of the budget?

11. Where will all the information for each section (Needs, Goals, Objectives, Logic Model, Budget, etc.) be derived from?

12. Who is in charge of being the grant lead and tying together the entire proposal?

13. When is the first rough draft deadline?

14. When is the deadline for the matching funds proof or letters?

15. When is the deadline for the budget?

16. Who will review the rough draft?

17. When is their deadline to return the rough draft to the grant writer?

18. When is the deadline for the second draft?

19. When is the deadline for the final draft? (Make sure this is NOT the deadline date for the grant.)

20. How many copies are needed, or how will the grant be submitted?

21. Are there any challenges foreseen when looking at the calendar? (i.e., Will anyone be on holiday when tasked with a responsibility, etc.)?

22. Who is the backup for submitting the grant?

For a downloadable template, please visit www.grantwritingandfunding.com/bookbonus.

Many of these questions may not make sense when writing a simple foundation grant, but believe me, they are vital for federal grants.

THE GRANT-WRITING STRUCTURE

Now, you know all there is to **set up your team.**

- ✓ **Grant team members**
- ✓ **A checklist of what needs to be discussed**

In Chapter Six, you learned that it is crucial to set up a grant team and delegate responsibilities. Remember, get your team together before you start writing the grant, and make sure you include the executive director, grant writing lead, budget lead, grant coordinator, and any specialist as part of this team. Furthermore, appoint someone (and a backup) to be in charge of submitting the grant application.

Another item to be mindful of is to actually read the entire FOA or RFP. These documents will provide exactly what to include in the grant application and often will even list the font, size, spacing, and number of pages for each section. If you do not adhere to these outlines, your precious grant could be rejected without even being read just because of formatting. Read the FOA or RFPs.

TIPS

✓ Have a kickoff grant meeting, and make sure all key people are tasked with responsibilities.

✓ Do not have too many different people write various sections without a grant lead to review all sections and ensure a cohesive grant.

✓ Make sure leadership tasks people with responsibilities!

✓ Read the entire FOA or RFP, and adhere to all guidelines and required attachments.

TOOLS

✓ To listen to more tips and information on grants, visit my podcast at www.grantwritingandfunding/podcast or subscribe on iTunes.

TEMPLATES

✓ For a checklist template for the grant kickoff meeting, visit www.grantwritingandfunding.com/bookbonus.

✓ For a grant timeline template, visit www.grantwritingandfunding.com/bookbonus.

NOTES:

SECTION 2:
"THE MAGIC"
G.R.A.N.T.S. FORMULA

Okay, we made it! We are at the apple pie filling of the book—the part you may have skipped to. The writing the structure of the grant part. This part is broken down into six sections:

- **G**et the FOA

- **R**esearch the Needs & Target Population

- **A**rticulate the Goals

- **N**arrow S.M.A.R.T. Objectives

- **T**imetable Your Activities

- **S**trategic Budgets

Once we have identified these key ingredients, we will focus on the final section: the narrative and creating credibility for your nonprofit.

Don't jump over the G.R.A.N.T.S. formula!

I know you are itching to write the narrative now, but this section will give you the entire structure to fill in the narrative and will essentially become the underlying structure.

The G.R.A.N.T.S. formula is what you will typically encounter when writing a grant. Some grants will ask for other specified information (some will ask for less), but most grantors will ask for the above information. The budget is frequently listed in the last section in grant applications, but I moved the budget up to provide a framework *before* you start your project narrative. You'll see why as you keep reading.

ALWAYS look at what the criteria are within the FOA or RFP (refer to the "G" of the G.R.A.N.T.S. formula). This information is to provide you with an outline so that you are ready to start formulating a grant. After finishing the grant-writing section, you will have a template to pull information from and apply to grants. When writing a grant, go straight to the grant-writing scoring section to see what is required. You must base your grant on what the funding source is asking. Remember, we aren't going down the entire "tomb" and "comb" differences and variations. For that, you can follow my podcast, Grant-Writing

Funding, at www.grantwritingandfunding.com/podcast or on SoundCloud (https://soundcloud.com/user-24992066-547781497) or iTunes (https://itunes.apple.com/us/podcast/grant-writing-funding/id1235917132?mt=2). I go into specifics and will answer your questions on my podcast.

In this section, you are going to learn how to outline a master template for a grant application. I encourage you to follow along and complete each section in this book. That way, when you find out about a perfect grant a week before it is due, you will be able to say, "Aha! I have a template already!" Won't that feel Zen?

You may already know what it feels like when you are not ready and your boss says there is a perfect grant available, but it is due in one week. That's when you end up pulling your hair out, ordering 10 espressos and pulling all-nighters. I've been there. I've gained five pounds in a week of grant writing deadlines as chocolate and coffee were the only things that would fuel me during those times. Really, we've all been there, right? Or am I the only one who used to have to lay on the floor and stare at a blank ceiling when things got overwhelming? Well, not any longer. And that is because I utilize the templates and the workbook that I am giving you. That's how they got created; I made these for order, productivity, and—let's face it—not to gain five pounds every time I write a grant!

CHAPTER SEVEN

G: GET THE FOA

Just what the heck is an FOA? you may be asking. Well, we touched base a bit about it above, but to reiterate, it stands for "Funding Opportunity Announcement." This is general lingo with federal grants, but other terms also include "Request For Proposal" (RFP) or "Request For Application" (RFA). Yes, as a grant writer, you will be able to wrap yourself in a blanket of acronyms.

My former boss and grant writer extraordinaire Dr. Jeffrey Rodman once said, "I just wrote an entire sentence using only acronyms." If you are from my generation of flip-phones, then you might be VERY familiar with using acronyms to save your thumb from getting sore when typing (if you are part of the iGen, you may not get this joke: JK, lol). But these acronyms for grants are still going strong nearly a quarter of the way through the new century.

This section will outline what FOAs and RFPs are, where you can find them, how they are different, and how to go from a blank page to an amazing grant template in a matter of seconds. Seconds? Yeah, seconds. Read on.

GET THE FOA OUTTA HERE!

The good ole FOA or RFP is the information published by the funding source that tells you how they want you to write the grant. For federal grants, you can find these listed on www.grants.gov.

Once you click on one that looks like it might be a good fit, your snapshot will look something like this:

BLM Funding Opportunity Announcement   No. L19AS00049

Project Title: BLM Utah Youth Conservation Opportunities on Public Lands   Page 1 of 46

BLM Utah Youth Conservation Opportunities on Public Lands

Notice of Funding Opportunity Number (NOFO): L19AS00049

Federal Program: 15.243 – BLM Youth Conservation Opportunities on Public Lands

Authorizing Legislation: Public Lands Corps Act of 1993, 16 USC, Chapter 37, Subchapter II-Public Lands Corps, Section 1721-1729, excluding Section 1725a Direct Hire Authority.

I. PROGRAM DESCRIPTION

The Utah Bureau of Land Management (BLM) offices have collaborated with Qualified Youth or Conservation Corps, as authorized by the Public Lands Corps Act (PLC), to accomplish conservation projects for numerous years. Projects completed under this program have provided participants an avenue of employment in addition to opportunities to gain experience and knowledge in public lands and natural resources management and promote a continued interest in public lands stewardship and the BLM. The BLM Youth Program assists the BLM with diversifying the workforce while exposing participants to the complex cultural and natural resource issues faced by managers of the National System for Public Lands.

The primary objective of the youth program is to work with Qualified Youth and Conservation Corps to engage individuals, to include tribal youth between the ages of 16 and 30, inclusive, and veterans age 35, recruited from local and surrounding communities to assist with completing projects that help protect and promote multiple-use conservation projects on public lands.

Projects made available under this funding announcement are developed in collaboration with the Utah Youth Program State Lead and District/Field Offices with an emphasis on providing valuable, on the ground projects, training, and mentorship opportunities to participants. The BLM Utah is committed to connecting diverse youth to public lands and natural and cultural heritage through providing conservation service projects, recreational experiences, and natural resource-based employment and educational opportunities, including scientific studies. These projects promote job creation that will strengthen America's economy and foster relationships with Youth Conservation Corps advocating for balanced stewardship and use of public lands. Participants will be mentored by BLM professionals in order to acquire new skills and gain experience in natural and cultural resource management. Through their BLM experience, youth will gain an appreciation for public lands, learn about conservation-related career fields, and create the next generation of public lands stewards.

In addition, the public will have improved access to sustainable recreation, hunting, and wildlife opportunities on BLM administered lands. Projects developed within this funding opportunity are in support of the following Secretarial Orders and Priorities:

Secretarial Orders:

- SO 3347 - Conservation Stewardship & Outdoor Recreation
- SO 3356 - Hunting, Fishing, Recreational Shooting & Wildlife Conservation Opportunities & Coordination with States, Tribes & Territories

FOAs are all VERY different. Each agency uses its own format. It is frustrating in the beginning, but, as you write grants, you get used to it. Much of the information is similar, but the format of the actual announcement is different. The view of the FOA you see in this book is very specific to the Department of the Interior, but even FOAs published under this agency can look very different. I don't want to add unnecessary pages to show you the full FOA (they can be extremely lengthy—upwards of 120 pages), so I encourage you to peruse www.grants.gov to get a feel for what the formats look like.

For foundation grants, it is a bit different. You can pay to use Foundation Directory Online, but you can also utilize GuideStar or Google. I know, I know, Googling foundations may be a little generic, but hey, it's free, and more and more foundations now have websites. I remember back in the day going into the Foundation Directory office in Washington, D.C., and using the various books to find the requirements of the grants and the physical addresses of foundations to then have to snail mail in applications. Eek. The job of grant research has definitely gotten a LOT easier with foundations getting and actually maintaining and updating their websites!

As mentioned, foundation FOAs or RFPs look different and have varying requirements. Some foundations want you to submit via an online application, and others (sigh, still) require a hard-copy application delivered. But most do ask for the same fundamental elements.

So, how do you save like a jillion hours and actually be "on point" when crafting your proposal when all FOAs and RFPs are, like, completely different?

Well, first, you actually have to READ the FOA or RFP. Yep, like go through it, and highlight and make notes. Figure out if your nonprofit is even eligible or competitive. For example, let's use the FOA from our youth search on Grants.gov about the National Park in Utah grant. If you have a youth soccer program 2,000 miles away from that specific National Park, then your nonprofit isn't a great fit.

Side note: Stop reading after the eligibility section, and delete the grant or send it to someone else who might be a good fit. Spend your time searching for better-fitting grants. Where many beginner grant writers waste their time is actually in the research. Instead of reading through the FOA, they jump right to the narrative section and start writing the grant. Several weeks later, and maybe 100 hours into working on a grant, they find out the nonprofit isn't even eligible. Ugh. Don't let that be you.

Back to our example.

However, if you have a youth empowerment program in the region adjacent to that National Park in Utah, keep reading.

If your nonprofit fits the eligibility and your project aligns with the priorities and the funding could benefit a project of yours, then download that FOA or RFP.

Look at the scoring criteria (usually toward the back in FOAs), and use the scoring criteria for your headers.

For an example of this, check out the RFP from Grant Writing & Funding, which funds our members!

(see below for what my RFP looks like for my Members Club!).

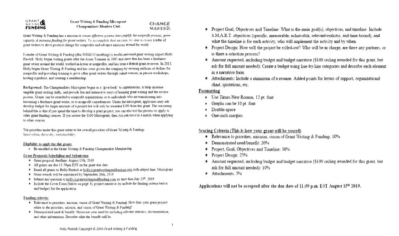

This is a micro-grant RFP that I released exclusively to my grant-writing members. (If you want more information on the Changemakers Members Club, check out www.grantwritingandfunding.com/members). This is an added benefit that my company provides to give newbie grant writers the opportunity to get experience writing grants, to get feedback on their grant application from yours truly, and to win a little cash. It is all a part of my mission to "grow capacity, increase funding, and advance mission!"

But enough shameless bragging. This activity is to show you how to go from blank page to grant template. Go to the scoring criteria portion of the RFP (see the close-up).

Scoring Criteria (This is how your grant will be scored)
- Relevance to priorities, mission, vision of Grant Writing & Funding: 10%
- Demonstrated need/benefit: 20%
- Project, Goal, Objectives and Timeline: 30%
- Project Design: 25%
- Amount requested, including budget and budget narrative ($100 ceiling awarded for this grant, but ask for full amount needed): 10%
- Attachments: 5%

Now, repurpose it for your template, like so…

Project Narrative

1. Relevance to GW&F priorities, mission, and vision
Here, review GW&F's priorities, mission, and vision, and align the nonprofit's project with each of these items.

2. Demonstrated Need and Benefits
Here, do research, and use stats to show the needs and also show the benefits to the community.

3. Project Goal, Objectives, and Timeline
Create a project goal that is related to a community goal. Create a S.M.A.R.T. objective, and include a timeline graph.

4. Project Design
How will the project roll out? Do we need to hire anyone? Who oversees whom? How will we select beneficiaries? Is there a sustainability model developed?

5. Amount Requested

How much do we need? Does it meet the cap of the grant? Are we leveraging any funds?

6. Attachments

Do we need to add any specific attachments such as resumes, letters of support, or IRS nonprofit status?

Now, you have a template for that specific grant. Trust me, federal grants will have many more headers and sub-headers, but this gives you a basic idea that will save you time and help YOU stay focused.

TIP: You can download the FOA or RFP and change it into a Word doc using an online free pdf2word converter.

Free online PDF to Word Doc Convertors (at the time of writing this book!):

https://pdf2doc.com/ or https://www.pdftoword.com/en/

G: GET THE FOA

In Chapter Seven, you learned it is imperative to get the FOA or RFP and *read it!* Then, you need to identify if you are even eligible to apply for the grant. If that is a hard "yes," then you now know how to utilize language from the FOA or RFP and use the scoring criteria for your headers.

Bang! In one swoop, you just went from blank page to a template for your grant. You also just made your grant more competitive than the next applicant who did not use this little magic trick, because you've made your grant easy to follow for the grant reviewers. Your template will follow the scoring pad that they follow.

Here is the checklist for getting the FOA or RFP and using it as a template

1. Read the entire FOA or RFP. (Yes, I did need to write that.)

2. Every grant is different! Remember this!

3. Keep all the items that are requested by the FOA or RFP, and use the criteria as headers in your application. If it is a federal grant, use the scoring criteria (usually towards the back) as the framework for ALL your headers.

CHAPTER EIGHT

R: RESEARCH THE NEEDS & TARGET DEMOGRAPHIC

For the rest of this book, we'll be using a (fictional) example to explore grant writing. Remember our soccer example with Charlene from Chapter Two: How to Think About Grants? Well, we'll be thinking about soccer again, but, instead of Charlene (the teenager who wants money for a soccer uniform), we are going to imagine that you are running a soccer program for disadvantaged youth in your community. If Charlene's parents didn't have enough money to fund Charlene's soccer uniforms and registration, your organization would be able to fund the entire kit and caboodle.

Let's call our fictional organization Youth Soccer Rocks. It's a nonprofit organization based in Rocking Socks City. (This is a fictional city—but wouldn't it be awesome if it were real??)

The Needs and Target Demographic section is the heart-wrenching part of your grant application. This is why your project needs to happen. It's the problem your project will be solving.

In this chapter, I will list

- ✓ how to articulate your target demographic,
- ✓ how to clearly state (and cite) your needs, and
- ✓ how to write a powerful problem statement.

This section will take a bit of time. You'll need to do the proper research and find updated statistics. You cannot just pull numbers out of the sky.

You may think, "Well, I know that the city of Rocking Socks has high poverty, so I will just write that." You are probably correct, but you need to reference a current source* to prove your point.

For instance, you can look at the U.S. Census to reference the number of households below the poverty line in Rocking Socks. You could also include information from newspapers, articles, surveys, community meetings (reference minutes of meetings), and so on.

Tip: A current source should be within the previous five years.

If you have a very specific niche, and it is truly difficult to find information within the previous five years, then you can break this rule of thumb. If you have a great source, but it's from 10 years ago, just make sure you explain why you are using the older source.

If you have a difficult time finding any information at all (and maybe that's why you are writing a grant so you can conduct a needs assessment to strengthen data in your area), then you can develop statistics. This doesn't mean you can manipulate information, but you can set up surveys, focus groups, social media polls, etc., to actually create statistics and data to demonstrate the need.

For example, you could conduct a survey for the youth in Rocking Socks City and ask if they are interested in attending soccer camps, what types of households they are from, or any other information that you may need. You could then include letters of testimony to show support, include graphs from the results of your surveys, and so forth. In this way, you are reaching out to your community to really find out the needs and then developing the best project to meet those needs. Additionally, you can utilize the research in your grants. *Voilà*!

I've got to say this research section has a way of going down a rabbit hole at times. Make sure that the needs section contains only information relevant for your project. For instance, it doesn't make sense if you include information and statistics about the elderly in your needs section (and take up precious pages in your grant application) if your entire project is about youth soccer.

This goes for your target demographic as well. The majority of your information should be based on your target demographic and not about the demographic at large. It may be important to first draw a brief overview of where your city is located and how many youths are in your community, but then, get to the point.

We often do this for the island of Guam, because, when you tell a lot of people you are from Guam, they ask, "who?"—not even where! But most organizations have nailed this down to a short paragraph so that the reviewers can understand the location and culture of the island. Once they have given general context to the location and culture, then they go deep into the specific target population and needs.

You can do this for your community because grant reviewers for federal grants are usually not from your community as this could constitute a conflict of interest. So, even though you think everyone should know about your location in Arkansas, you might be wrong; there are even grant reviewers on the island of Guam (wink, wink) who have no idea about the overall regional needs of Arkansas.

Furthermore, most grant applications have very specific page limitations, so you really don't want to waste pages on unnecessary information. Another thing to consider is that grant reviewers may be tired by the time they get to your application. If they can't easily identify a clear problem and the target demographic to be served, they may reduce points. Take note that grant reviewers are just people, and they review a lot of grants in a very short period of time!

Let's use the Youth Soccer Rocks example to get some ideas on how to fill out this section for your specific organization.

> *"Do not use the terms 'Lack of' or 'Need for.'*
> *Do discuss the current conditions."*
>
> ~ ADMINISTRATION FOR NATIVE AMERICANS Application Toolkit

PROBLEM OR NEED

Be very specific when articulating needs. For example, if you just state that there is a lack of soccer programs in the community, it does not really demonstrate a problem, and it is very abstract. A lack could mean there are five other soccer programs or no other soccer programs. Through your research, you may find out that there are no other soccer organizations or that there are other soccer organizations, but they require participant fees. In this case, you could state,

"There are no free soccer programs available to youth in Rocking Socks City."

That is clear.

Another reoccurring fault by many organizations in the needs section is listing the solutions.

They may state something like,

"There is a need for soccer programs in our city."

Just because you are using the word "need" doesn't mean you are identifying a need. You are actually showing a solution here. Do you see that?

You have to show why having no free soccer programs in your community is a problem. Your research may have provided information such as a high prevalence of at-risk youth who are overweight and have type 2 diabetes in your community. This is a problem and is a current condition.

Your actual problem statement could be,

"75% of at-risk youth in the city of Rocking Socks suffer from chronic health issues compared to the national average of 12%."

Do you see how this is a current condition that is very specific and how your project is then the solution to solve this problem or need?

TARGET DEMOGRAPHIC

The target demographic is usually a much easier concept. It simply states who you will serve. Sometimes, you will be serving all in the community with specific projects, but often, you will be serving a particular segment of the population. By narrowing down a specific portion of the population, you will have a little more control over the results. This goes back to even finding grants. You don't just apply for all grants; you find out which ones will be the best fit for your organization. In the same way, you will want to know who your organization is specifically serving.

GET TO WORK

What is the problem? It's okay to start with something general.

e.g., There are a lot of youth in Rocking Socks that are at risk for health issues.

Write your response:

_____

_____

_____

_____

_____

_____

_____

Who is your target population/demographic?

e.g., Youth Soccer Rocks serves the underserved youth ages 14- to 26-years-old who are at risk for health issues in Rocking Socks City.

Write your response:

_____

_____

_____

_____

_____

_____

_____

What do you want to change?

e.g., We want to reduce the number of youth with obesity and diabetes in our community by 25%.

Write your response:

_____

_____

_____

_____

_____

_____

_____

Where are some places you could find data or statistics to support the problem?

e.g., The U.S. Census, the Internet, the Rocking Socks newspapers, surveys at Rocking Socks schools, minutes of meetings from board meetings and community meetings, etc.

Write your response:

_____

_____

_____

_____

_____

_____

Find statistics and data to back up your problem/need. If you need to take some time and research, go ahead. Then, come back and enter information. Put down the source, year, and URL (if found online).

Reminder: This can be research curated from the Internet, the U.S. Census, newspaper articles, scholarly journals and articles, interviews, focus groups, surveys, questionnaires, data reported from similar organizations, etc. Try to use sources that are dated no more than five years before your current date. Very niched information or genres may not have updated information, so you may need to use documentation that is more than five years old. Just be sure to describe why it is difficult to obtain your statistics or data.

Write your response:

_____

_____

_____

_____

_____

Articulate one clear problem/need statement, not just a solution.

e.g., Do not merely state, "Soccer for youth in Rocking Socks City will create a positive outlet and decrease health risks." That is a vague solution that may go in a different section of your grant.

Write your response:

_____

_____

_____

_____

_____

Get more precise on your problem:

e.g., 75% of youth in the city of Rocking Socks suffer from chronic health issues compared to the national average of 12%. These staggering health issues correlate with high suicide rates, depression rates, and poor graduation rates.

Write your response:

_____

_____

_____

_____

_____

_____

_____

Create a clear problem/need sentence:

e.g., There are no free soccer programs in the Rocking Socks region. According to Rocking Socks Consolidated Health Report (2016), 75% of youth ages 14- to 26-years-old are below the poverty level in Rocking Socks City.

Write your response:

_____

_____

_____

_____

_____

_____

_____

For a downloadable template on needs and target demographics, visit
www.grantwritingandfunding.com/bookbonus.

R: RESEARCH THE NEEDS & TARGET DEMOGRAPHIC

To articulate specific needs and the target demographic, be clear. In this chapter, we articulated your target demographic, how to clearly state (and cite) needs, and how to write a powerful problem statement.

You learned how to identify and state your needs and that, to adequately reference the needs in the community, you must utilize information, statistics, and data from the previous five years. As a reminder, if recent citations or references are difficult to find, then start coordinating efforts to support your needs, such as conducting surveys, focus groups, or meetings or gathering testimonials.

For your target demographic, make sure you are clearly serving one area. Yes, certain projects may serve an entire community, but be sure to clearly explain that community and that they have a common need. Be clear and precise with this section.

Use quantitative and qualitative information to demonstrate the issues. For example, you can use numbers and percentages to identify the unemployment rate over the last few years compared to that of the entire nation. At the same time, you could also include an example of some of the youth you served and how they couldn't pay for socks and shoes and came from Child Protective Services (of course, omitting names) to really give a face to the statistics. Make sure you are clearly showing the need and who you will serve and not the solution. The goals, objectives, and projective design will all talk about your solution.

TIPS:

✓ A current source should be within the previous five years.

✓ Clearly describe your problem and your target demographic.

✓ Create data by implementing a Needs & Strengths Assessment.

TOOLS

For data and statistics across the nation, visit

✓ https://www.census.gov/

✓ https://www.usa.gov/statistics

TEMPLATES

✓ For a downloadable template on needs and target demographics, visit www.grantwritingandfunding.com/bookbonus.

✓ For a grant timeline template, visit www.grantwritingandfunding.com/bookbonus.

NOTES:

CHAPTER NINE

A: ARTICULATE YOUR GOAL

"Setting goals is the first step in turning the invisible into the visible."

~ TONY ROBBINS

Having an overarching articulated goal is vital to guide your grant. Sure, you may have more than one goal, but I recommend (especially for smaller grants) having only one. In this way, all of your objectives (we'll get to those in the next chapter) will be the roadmap on reaching your goal. But just like having a vision for your nonprofit that shows where the road will end, a goal shows the overall impact of your grant project. Once you know your problem statement (from the previous section), you can figure out your goal.

The best goals relate to a community outcome and demonstrate a behavior change. This is not an objective. We will get into that in a minute. Goals are the big, overarching aim of what your project hopes to achieve in the long term.

How to develop a goal:

- ✓ Draft your project idea.
- ✓ Who/what is your target population to be served?
- ✓ What is the main problem your project will solve?
- ✓ What is the main change you want to see?
- ✓ How does your project align with a community outcome?
- ✓ Flip your problem statement around.

Your project idea

e.g., Youth Soccer Nonprofit wants to develop a soccer program for at-risk youth.

Now, draft your project idea:

_____

_____

_____

_____

_____

_____

_____

_____

Who/what is your target population to be served?

e.g., At-risk youth ages 12- to 18-years-old who are at risk for type II diabetes in Rocking Socks city.

Write your target population to be served:

_____

_____

_____

_____

_____

_____

_____

_____

What is the main problem that will be solved?

e.g., Chronic health issues will be reduced by 50% for underserved youth.

Write your response:

_____

_____

_____

_____

_____

_____

_____

What is the main change you want to see?

e.g., Provide a pathway for low-income youth with risk factors of getting type II diabetes to be healthy.

Write the main change you want your project to implement:

_____

_____

_____

_____

_____

_____

_____

What larger community outcome can you integrate into your larger goal? (This can be mission statements from larger organizations, community plans, etc.)

e.g., The Rocking Socks City Council Consolidated Plan includes access to health for all.

Write your response:

_____

_____

_____

_____

_____

_____

_____

Rewrite your problem statement.

e.g., There are no free soccer programs in the Rocking Socks region. According to Rocking Socks Consolidated Health Report (2016), 75% of youth ages 14- to 26-years-old are below the poverty level in Rocking Socks City.

_____

_____

_____

_____

_____

_____

For your goal, you will flip it around, i.e., what will be changed?

e.g., Youth Soccer Rocks will provide a free soccer program for at-risk youth and provide a pathway to health.

Write your response:

_____

_____

_____

_____

_____

_____

_____

_____

A: ARTICULATE YOUR GOAL

In Chapter Nine, you learned why an overarching articulated goal is vital to guide your grant and how to create one. You also saw why the best goals relate to a community outcome and demonstrate a behavior change.

Now, you know how to easily develop a goal:

- ✓ Draft your project idea
- ✓ Articulate who/what is your target population to be served
- ✓ Articulate what the main problem is that your project will solve
- ✓ Articulate what the main change is that you want to see
- ✓ Articulate how your project aligns with a community goal
- ✓ Articulate your goal by flipping around your problem statement

It's really pretty, right? This great goal in the sky—but how do you reach your goal?

By creating objectives… .

TIPS

✓ Flip around your problem statement to craft a powerful and articulate goal.

TOOLS

✓ **Use the following process to identify your goal:**

- Draft your project idea.
- Who/what is your target population to be served?
- What is the main problem your project will solve?
- What is the main change you want to see?
- How does your project align with a community outcome?

TEMPLATES

✓ None.

NOTES:

CHAPTER TEN

N: NARROW S.M.A.R.T. OBJECTIVES

"Management by objectives works—if you know the objectives.
Ninety percent of the time, you don't."

~ PETER DRUCKER

Objectives are the backbone of your project. A grant is like a big jigsaw puzzle, and this section is really the backdrop and what guides you to be able to find and connect each piece of the puzzle. It's the fence in the background in your puzzle or the house with the clean line, the image you use as a guide to connect the pieces. If you have your objective, you will be able to formulate a budget, implement activities, and solve your problem by reaching your goal.

In this chapter, you will learn

- ✓ how to write S.M.A.R.T. objectives and
- ✓ how to write measured outcomes.

Think of objectives as the specific framework of what will be accomplished. Typically, you do not want to have any more than three objectives within a project. You will have many activities, but the overall objectives should be clear and concise. Objectives need to be S.M.A.R.T.: specific, measurable, achievable, relevant, and time-bound.

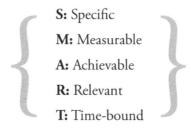

S: Specific

M: Measurable

A: Achievable

R: Relevant

T: Time-bound

What is your objective? Is it S.M.A.R.T.?

e.g., Objective (1): 100 disadvantaged youth in Rocking Socks will receive sports scholarships by the end of 12 months.

Let's break this down into each part of the S.M.A.R.T acronym. By the end, you will have one entire objective.

Specific: Identify the outcomes that will be achieved:

e.g., Number of youth, type of youth, what their specific outcome will be.

_____

_____

_____

_____

_____

_____

_____

_____

Measurable: Use quantifiable terms to describe how the progress will be measured.

e.g., Number of youth (100) and number of scholarships.

_____

_____

_____

_____

_____

_____

_____

_____

Achievable: Is the objective achievable within the duration of the project, resources, budget, etc.?

e.g., This would be balanced by the needs, i.e., If there are thousands of youth who are disadvantaged in the city and no other free soccer organizations, then this could be achievable.

_____

_____

_____

_____

_____

_____

Relevant: Does the objective relate to the problem statement and goal?

e.g., This is a possible solution to the health conditions.

_____

_____

_____

_____

_____

_____

Time-bound: Do you have a date for the objective to be completed by? Tip: Start off with the end in the beginning of the objective, such as, "By the end of 12 months…"

e.g., They will complete this objective by the end of 12 months.

_____

_____

_____

_____

_____

_____

_____

_____

Okay, now, put an objective together, and use this activity for further objectives. What is your objective? Is it S.M.A.R.T.?

e.g., Objective (1): 100 disadvantaged youth in Rocking Socks will receive sport scholarships by the end of 12 months.

_____

_____

_____

_____

_____

_____

_____

OUTCOMES

"To conquer frustration, one must remain intensely focused on the outcome, not on the obstacles."

~ T. F. HODGE

The outcomes are what will specifically be accomplished. Include your baseline and how data will be tracked to communicate your outcomes.

What are your outcomes?

e.g., At the beginning of the project, there are zero sports scholarships available to disadvantaged youth in Rocking Socks. By the end of year one, 100 youth will have received sports scholarships and participated in health checks. We will track the number of scholarships delivered and the number of youth participating in the health checks via a roster sheet.

Write your response:

_____

_____

_____

_____

_____

_____

_____

_____

_____

_____

_____

_____

_____

_____

_____

_____

_____

_____

N: NARROW S.M.A.R.T. OBJECTIVES

In Chapter Ten, you learned that objectives are the backbone of your project, and it is super vital to narrow them down using the S.M.A.R.T. process. Remember, a grant is like a big jigsaw puzzle, and your objectives really provide the backdrop and what guides you to be able to find and connect each piece of the puzzle.

You learned how to ensure that each objective is S.M.A.R.T.:

Specific

Measurable

Achievable

Relevant

Time-bound

You also learned how to identify an outcome of each objective. Do you know see how your objectives really lay out the process for reaching your goal?

But Holly, there are more steps to achieve the objective! I know, I know—that is why we are going to talk about the next steps that will help you reach your objectives. Do you see how this is really just layers on top of layers? The top layer is the problem; then, we peel back a layer and see the large goal. Then, we peel back a few layers to see the objectives. Next, we peel back some more layers to see the activities....

TIPS

✓ Objectives need to be S.M.A.R.T.: specific, measurable, achievable, relevant, and time-bound.

✓ Start or end your objective with it being time-bound, such as: By the end of 12 months…

TOOLS

✓ **Use each word from the S.M.A.R.T. acronym to figure out if your objectives are comprehensive.**

S: Specific

M: Measurable

A: Achievable

R: Relevant

T: Time-bound

TEMPLATES

✓ None.

NOTES:

_____
_____
_____
_____
_____
_____
_____
_____
_____
_____
_____
_____
_____
_____
_____
_____
_____
_____
_____
_____
_____
_____
_____
_____
_____
_____
_____
_____
_____
_____
_____
_____

CHAPTER ELEVEN

T: TIMETABLE YOUR ACTIVITIES

"Empower your dreams with deadlines."

~ H. JACKSON BROWN, JR.

One of the most important items you can create in the design process of writing a grant is to formulate a timetable. The timetable is not only helpful for scoring higher on grant applications; it is also super helpful for YOU when the grant is funded. You will need to know what to do, when to do it, and who will do it.

In this chapter, you will learn

✓ how to outline all of your activities to stay on track,

✓ how to ensure all items needed to meet your objectives are included,

✓ how to identify who is responsible for each activity, and

✓ how to safeguard that all your activities are timebound.

Activities describe what you are going to do, but a timetable will show a clear delineation of each activity, who is responsible for ensuring that it happens, when it will happen, and how each activity will be measured. All activities should be connected to your S.M.A.R.T. objectives.

By providing a timetable for your activities, you are demonstrating that each activity will actually happen and how each one leads to making sure your objective is reached. This timetable ALSO is a great table to break up all the WORDS in your application. This timetable will definitely help your grant stand out compared to others who list activities in a narrative.

Include the following:

1. **Description of activity:** This is the basic description of the activity to be accomplished.
2. **Lead person who will be responsible for the activity:** This is the main person responsible for ensuring that the activity is done.
3. **Start date of activity:** This is when the activity will start.
4. **End date of activity:** This is when the activity will be done.

This is the format for how you can include activities. Remember, use a graph if you can as it helps break up the words and gets your point across quickly and clearly.

Once this is created, your project is a legacy. What do I mean by that? Well, you should be able to hand over the timeline and budget to someone who gets hired from the grant, and they should be able to run the project with minimal further direction. Sure, you will want a handoff meeting and all that fun stuff, but if they have this piece in their arsenal, they can keep referring to it to stay on track with the implementation of the project. This is awesome. Remember to include items from the budget in your timeline. ***For a downloadable template, go to* www.grantwritingandfunding.com/bookbonus.**

Problem Statement: There are no free soccer programs in Rocking Socks region. According to Rocking Socks Consolidated Health Report (2016), 75% of youth ages 14- to 26-years-old are below the poverty level in Rocking Socks City.

Goal: Youth Soccer Rocks will provide a free soccer program for at-risk youth and provide a healthy pathway to help reduce and prevent obesity and health concerns for at-risk youth.

Objective: 100 disadvantaged youth in Rocking Socks will receive sports scholarships by the end of 12 months.

ACTIVITY	PERSON RESPONSIBLE/LEAD	START DATE	END DATE
Kickoff Meeting	Executive Director/BOD	Oct. 1, 2019	Oct. 1, 2019
Recruit Project Manager	Executive Director	Oct. 7, 2019	Oct. 21, 2019
Hire Project Manager	Executive Director	Oct. 22, 2019	Oct. 25, 2019
Buy computer	Project Manager	Oct. 30, 2019	Oct. 30, 2019
Community Outreach	Project Manager	Oct. 31, 2019	Nov. 30, 2019
Connect with Partners at quarterly meeting	ED and PM	Dec. 7, 2019	Dec. 7, 2019
Select 100 youth participants	ED and PM	Dec. 20, 2019	Jan. 5, 2020
Buy soccer uniforms	PM	Jan. 8, 2020	Jan. 10, 2020
Soccer camp	Coach	Jan. 20, 2020	Feb. 20, 2020
Attend required grant meeting	PM and Bookkeeper	March 1, 2020	March 3, 2020

Your turn. Fill out the following action plan timeline.

PROBLEM STATEMENT:			
GOAL:			
OBJECTIVE:			
ACTIVITY	PERSON RESPONSIBLE/LEAD	START DATE	END DATE

T: TIMETABLE YOUR ACTIVITIES

In this chapter, you learned how to timetable your activities. You now have a workable tool, the action plan timetable, to implement all your activities.

This is really the part where your entire grant team needs to be on board—this part coupled with the budget. Once you have this information, the rest can be done with follow-up meetings, emails, and phone calls. Make sure your goals, objectives, and outcomes are all solutions to your problem. You would be surprised, but sometimes, FOAs or RFPs do not request any or all of this information. My advice to you: include it anyway if you have the space.

As you can tell, your goal, objectives, and outcomes could probably all be included in one paragraph or in bullet points. But just because they are short doesn't mean they aren't well thought out. So, even if a funding source doesn't request this information, if you provide it, and it weaves your entire proposal together seamlessly, you will be ahead of those who don't include it.

Now, you know how to outline all of your activities in a really cool way. You timetable shows a clear delineation of each activity, who is responsible for ensuring that it happens, and when it will happen. All activities are connected to your S.M.A.R.T. objectives, your goal, and your problem statement!

By providing a timetable for your activities, you have demonstrated that each activity will actually happen and how each one leads to making sure your objective is reached.

TIPS

✓ Make sure you list all the activities needed to reach your objective.

✓ Use a timetable to create more dimension within your grant application.

TOOLS

✓ Utilize the Timetable in the Templates.

TEMPLATES

✓ For a downloadable template of the Timetable for Activities, visit www.grantwritingandfunding.com/bookbonus.

NOTES:

CHAPTER TWELVE

S: STRATEGIC BUDGETS

Cha-Ching. It's time to talk about the money. The budget. This is often the weakest section of grant applications, perhaps because it is usually one of the last items listed in the FOA or RFP. But this should not be the last section you write. You should write this section in alignment with the objectives and your activities—which is precisely why I've placed it right after the Activities chapter.

If you have an activity in the timetable, then you should see if it should be in the budget. This way, you keep the entire design extremely clear, and the project will have the needed money to implement activities. If you design the objectives, activities, and budget properly, your project narrative should flow naturally and easily. Always think of the activities and budget like a healthy marriage.

Many grant writers will use the excuse that they are word-savvy but aren't good with numbers while fiscal agents will say the opposite. However, to be a good grant writer, you must be good with both words and numbers. You will have to turn the numbers into words within your budget narrative justification.

In this chapter, you will learn how to write a strategic budget and budget narrative in the format that grant reviewers appreciate. You will know which budget category to put each item in and how to calculate costs. You will also get links to resources to help you put a reliable cost on each item.

The good news is that you don't have to be a CPA to write a budget. You do, however, need to *understand* budgets. I know I've picked on small nonprofits, but now, it's time to reverse roles as this section is where smaller nonprofits sometimes thrive. Why? A lot of times, project managers have to understand budgets because there may not be a full-time bookkeeper or finance division. Larger organizations will have an entirely separate financial division, and, while this is great (and essential), it can also hinder the philosophy of viewing a grant in its totality. Larger organizations will have a programmatic division and a separate finance division. This is not always a good thing as they may not communicate efficiently. For example, the fiscal division may not be involved when it comes to the design of grants because this is assumed to be more programmatic.

I urge you, no matter the size of your organization, to have both sides of the coin (programmatic and finance) sit at the table during the grant design planning stage of writing up the objectives, timeline, and budget. (Remember how to develop a Grant Team?) Don't segregate this process! You need everyone on the same page.

Outlining the objectives, timeline, and budget can sometimes only take a matter of a couple of hours. Seriously! This input and mindset can save your organization literally hundreds of hours. I have experienced the difference first hand.

As a grant-writing consultant, I have been a part of the process for many different organizations with various mindsets of grant writing, and I know how much easier it is—and how much time is saved—when applying this grant-writing process.

Side note: It is a little ironic that many people think of grants somewhat like lottery money, but if you use the word "budget" in regular life, people cringe and think of deprivation.

BUDGET CATEGORIES

The following is an outline of the main budget categories. Think of these categories as the main framework for your budget. These will be the main categories that I will use in all templates. Of course, your organization may add subcategories (the items under the main categories), and that is perfectly fine—but this is to provide you with a general framework for your budget.

Budget Categories:

- Personnel
- Fringe Benefits
- Travel
- Contracts/Consultants
- Equipment
- Supplies
- Other
- Indirect

HOW MUCH DO YOU ASK FOR?

Just like your objective needs to be S.M.A.R.T., so does your budget. Your budget also needs to be specific, measurable, achievable, relevant, and time-bound.

Specific: Don't fall into the trap of using the word "miscellaneous" for a budget subcategory. Be specific when listing all your subcategories. *e.g., Full-time Employee (FTE) Project Director.*

Measurable: If you utilize the budget template within this book, then you will be able to adhere to measuring your budget appropriately. This is under the computation column of the budget. *e.g., FTE Project Director at 2080 hours × $25 per hour = $52,000.*

Achievable: To ensure that your budget items are achievable, your budget needs to make sense. Is there enough work for your project director to be hired on a full-time basis if you only offer one summer camp a year for two weeks? On the flip side, do you have ample resources included in your budget to meet the objectives?

If there is a required training for two staff members to attend a three-day training in Washington, D.C., and your organization is based in California, would you only include $100 for the training in the budget? No, you wouldn't (or, if you really could, please give me your travel agent's name and number ASAP!).

Relevant: If you put your timeline next to your budget and are sure that each item is accounted for, then your budget should be relevant. If you listed hiring a project director in your timeline and discussed the project director's role in your project design, then it would be relevant to include a project director in your budget. On the other hand, if you did not include the project director in your timeline or project design, then it would not be completely relevant to include one in your budget.

Time-bound: Your budget is usually listed year by year or for a certain duration. Even if you are applying for a three-year federal grant, they are going to want to see the budget broken down year by year. If you break down your personnel computations on an annual basis but then clump all your rent or supplies into three years, it will be confusing for the reviewer. Some grant periods are less than a year and only for a specific season. Therefore, it is important to pay attention to the duration and when the grant will be awarded. That way, you can be more specific with scheduling the grant budget so it makes sense.

Do you have a line-by-line budget? (Check one)

Yes _____ No _____ Not Sure _____

For a line-by-line budget template, visit www.grantwritingandfunding.com/bookbonus.

PERSONNEL

Let's start with personnel. Usually, you will need to contact the accounting department for this information. Take note that, in the case of a multi-year grant, many organizations have automatic percentage increases each year for their employees. If not, it is still a good practice to allow for inflation and give a small percentage increase for most items each year.

You will want to include the staff that will be working on the grant project in this section. This may include positions that have not been hired yet, and that is fine. Make sure you include updated resumes and job descriptions for all personnel that you will hire as employees for the grant project (Refer to Chapter Seven). If you will be hiring a completely new position, make sure you include a new job description for this position.

How much should the wages be? This is a grant, so you can jack up all the salaries at any amount, right? Nope. Be careful here. The best practice is to use the Department of Labor's wage and hour determination. Visit https://www.dol.gov/whd/ for more information for your specific state. Not all job titles will be included in these databases, but you can use a job that has similar educational or training qualifications. If you do increase an employee's salary in a drastic way (specifically the executive director), make sure this is done by a vote from the board of directors before the wage is changed.

Take a moment to fill this section out even if you aren't sure of all the different personnel who will be hired. *Note: You can include the executive director as key personnel, but I encourage you to only include a percentage of their time as grants generally fund projects and not entire budgets of organizations. This goes for bookkeepers and other administration as well. Some organizations include all executive levels and administration as a part of their indirect costs to streamline cost allocations.*

PERSONNEL				
POSITION TITLE	COMPUTATION (HOURLY RATE × # OF HOURS)	GRANT REQUEST TOTAL	MATCHING	TOTAL
e.g., Director	($35 per hour × 2080 hours) × 30%	$21,840		$21,840
Project Manager	$25 per hour × 2080 hours	$52,000		$52,000
Coach	$20 per hour × 560 hours		$11,200	$11,200
Bookkeeper	($15 per hour × 1040 hours) × 20%	$3,120		$3,120
Personnel Subtotal	The sum of all personnel	$76,960	$11,200	$88,160

Budget Narrative: Example

Executive Director: Youth Soccer Rocks will allocate 30% of the executive director's time towards this project at $35 per hour for 2080 hours, totaling $21,840. The executive director will oversee and compile reports and supervise the project manager, coach, and bookkeeper.

Project Manager: Youth Soccer Rocks will have a full-time project manager at $25 per hour for 2080 hours, totaling $52,000. The project manager will oversee all aspects of the project and will report directly to the executive director. The project manager will interact with all partners and will monitor all nonfederal matching partners to ensure that they are meeting their commitments. The project manager will also oversee the contractor and ensure that all outreach and awareness material advertisements are completed.

Coach: The coach will volunteer his/her time to coach the soccer team three times a week during the soccer season and at games for $20 per hour × 560 hours, totaling $11,200. See attached the signed letter of commitment from the coach.

Bookkeeper: The bookkeeper will oversee all financial accounts for the project and will submit financial reports to the executive director as well as attend the required training. He/she will work part-time at $15 per hour for 1,040 hours, totaling $3,120.

Grant Request Total: $76,960

Nonfederal Total: $11,200

Total Personnel: $88,160

Now your turn:

PERSONNEL				
POSITION TITLE	COMPUTATION (HOURLY RATE × # OF HOURS)	GRANT REQUEST TOTAL	MATCHING	TOTAL
Personnel Subtotal	The sum of all personnel			

Budget Narrative: Write out each role, the computation, and job description.

Write your response:

_____

_____

_____

_____

_____

_____

_____

_____

_____

Grant Request Total: _____

Nonfederal Total: _____

Total Personnel: _____

FRINGE BENEFITS

Fringe benefits vary from organization to organization except for the Federal Insurance Contributions Act (FICA) rate, which is made up of two items: Social Security and Medicare taxes. For 2019, the Social Security tax rate is 6.2% on the first $127,200 wages paid. The Medicare tax rate is 1.45% on the first $200,000 and 2.35% above $200,000. Most of the time, the FICA rate you will use is 7.65% (although this can change, so make sure you stay up to date). All other fringe benefits vary from state to state and from organization to organization.

A cautionary note: Make sure you are following your contract and grant requirements. For instance, some state contracts may require that you include health and welfare for your employees, and they will include a specific rate. Read your contracts, and make sure you incorporate all requirements.

Let's go ahead and start with the Youth Soccer Rocks example.

FRINGE BENEFITS				
FRINGE BENEFITS	RATE	GRANT REQUEST TOTAL	MATCHING	TOTAL
FICA	Multiply the total of the personnel salary by 7.65%	$5,887	$857	$6,744
Workers Comp	Multiply the total by 1.5%	$1,154	$168	$1,322
Health Insurance	Each full-time person receives $350 per month	$5,460	$-	$5,460
Fringe Benefits Subtotal		$12,502	$1,025	$13,527

Budget Narrative: Example

FICA: The FICA rate is at 7.65%: $5,887 for grant-requested salaries and $857 for nonfederal personnel salaries, totaling $6,744.

Workers Compensation: The Workers Compensation Rate is 1.5%: $1,154 for grant-requested salaries and $168 for nonfederal matching, totaling $1,322.

Health Insurance: Health insurance is only for full-time employees for $350 per month. This grant will cover $5,460 of full-time employees only, which are all grant-requested personnel.

Grant Request Total: $12,502

Nonfederal Total: $1,025

Total Fringe Benefits: $13,527

Now your turn:

FRINGE BENEFITS				
FRINGE BENEFITS	RATE	GRANT REQUEST TOTAL	MATCHING	TOTAL
FICA				
Unemployment				
Workers Comp				
Retirement				
Health Insurance				
Fringe Benefits Subtotal				

Budget Narrative: Describe fringe benefits and the computation.

Write your response:

_____

_____

_____

_____

_____

_____

_____

_____

Grant Request Total: _____

Nonfederal Total: _____

Total Fringe Benefits: _____

TRAVEL

Travel will be divided into actual travel for conferences and trips and general around-town types of travel. For example, Youth Soccer Rocks will have one grant-required training to attend in Washington, D.C., which the project manager and accountant will attend. They will also include gas mileage for using the minivan to transport kids to soccer games. Make sure you include any required travel in your grants. Also, if you state that your staff will attend other regional trainings, then include that in your budget and in your timeline.

Traveling to conferences and trainings needs to be specific. You will need to include the costs of lodging, flights or trains (if necessary), rental cars (if necessary), and per diem. Don't try to pull these numbers out of the air. You can easily visit https://www.gsa.gov to get the meals and incidental rates and lodging for virtually every city in the United States. *Note: Meals & Incidentals are at 75% of total daily costs when traveling to and from the destination. For example, if you flew out from California on a Monday to Washington, D.C., and the conference started on Tuesday, you would get 75% of the total meals and incidental costs for the day you were traveling.*

For flights: You may need to find three separate quotes and include the lowest cost or the one that will have adequate arrival and departure times. For example, if the cheapest flight was only $100 less but the departure time for the training delayed you for an additional day, you would need to include another day for lodging and per diem, which would probably be more than $100. Therefore, use common sense when booking your flight, but be sure to explain why you are taking the "expensive" flight. Got it?

Also, I have included the option for a rental car within this budget. You don't always need to rent a car. Sometimes, you will be staying at the same hotel as the conference or would rather walk or take public transportation. Once again, figure out what makes sense. At the same time, if you need the rental car, include it.

For general driving costs, you can include the IRS standard mileage rates. This can change year to year, so make sure that you take a look at this every year to find out if the rate has changed. Just see how often gas prices fluctuate! Federal grants will usually only approve the maximum amount as included in this rate. The 2019 rate is $0.58 per mile. Visit the IRS website for updated information: https://www.gsa.gov/travel/plan-book/transportation-airfare-rates-pov-rates/privately-owned-vehicle-pov-mileage-reimbursement-rates.

TRAVEL*				
TYPE	COMPUTATION	GRANT REQUEST TOTAL	MATCHING	TOTAL
Conference/ Required Training	Required Grant in D.C. in January			
Airfare	$500 × 2 people	$1,000	$-	$1,000
Lodging	$182 per day for 3 nights for 2 people	$1,092	$-	$1,092
Meals & Incidentals	$69 per day for 3 days for 2 people + $51.75 for two days of traveling	$621	$-	$621
Mileage for Driving for Work	Driving kids to soccer—average 100 miles per week × 52 weeks × $.535 per mile.	$-	$2,782	$2,782
Travel Subtotal	Add up everything	$2,713	$2,782	$5,495

Budget Narrative: Example

Required Training: Youth Soccer Rocks will have the project manager and bookkeeper attend the required conference in Washington, D.C. The current airfare price from Soccer Rocks' state to Washington, D.C., is $500. Therefore, we will have two people taking round-trip flights at $1,000. Lodging, based on the GSA estimates, will be $182 per night for two people, totaling $1,092. Meals and Incidentals, based on current GSA estimates, will be $69 per day for three days for two people plus $51.75 for two days of traveling, totaling $621. All required training costs will be grant requested at $2,713.

Mileage for Driving: Youth Soccer Rocks will transport all youth to soccer practices, games, and related activities. We estimate that this will be 100 miles per week for 52 weeks at the federal mileage cost of $.535 per mile, totaling $2,782. This cost will be covered by a nonfederal grant.

Grant Request Total: $2,713

Nonfederal Total: $2,782

Total Travel: $5,495

Now, your turn:

TRAVEL*				
TYPE	COMPUTATION	GRANT REQUEST TOTAL	MATCHING	TOTAL
Conference/ Required Training	Name of training			
Airfare	Cost of flight × number of individuals			
Lodging	Costs of hotel × number of nights × number of people			
Meals & Incidentals	Daily per diem rate × number of days × number of people			
Ground Transportation	Daily rental car costs × number of days × number of people			
Mileage for Driving for Work	Average number of miles × federal rate.			
Travel Subtotal	Add up everything			

Budget Narrative: Write out the description for travel.

Write your response:

_____

_____

_____

_____

_____

Grant Request Total: _____

Nonfederal Total: _____

Total Travel:_____

EQUIPMENT

This category can be a little confusing as a lot of organizations want to include computers and cellphones. That might work for a foundation grant, but if you are considering federal grants, then adhere to the federal requirements. According to the Federal Uniform Guidelines in the Code of Federal Regulations, equipment is defined as

"tangible personal property (including information technology systems) having a useful life of more than one year and a per-unit acquisition cost which equals or exceeds the lesser of the capitalization level established by the nonfederal entity for financial statement purposes, or $5,000." 2 CFR 200.33

What this means in laymen's terms is that any item (not separate items that surpass $5,000 when combined, but a singular item) that will be $5,000 or more and has the lifespan of more than one year is considered equipment. I would suggest listing at least three quotes to show that you are getting the best deal on the equipment.

e.g., Youth Soccer Rocks will allocate federal funds from this grant to purchase a minivan.

EQUIPMENT				
ITEMS	COMPUTATION	GRANT REQUEST TOTAL	MATCHING	TOTAL
One Minivan	Purchasing a minivan	$20,000	$-	$20,000
Equipment Subtotal		$20,000	$-	$20,000

Budget Narrative: Example

Minivan: Youth Soccer Rocks requests the purchase of a seven-seater minivan at $20,000. The minivan is essential for driving our youth to soccer games, practices, and related activities. See three quotes of minivans to ensure the most economical cost for the minivan, totaling $20,000.

Grant Request Total: $20,000

Nonfederal Total: $0

Total Equipment: $20,000

Now, your turn.

EQUIPMENT				
ITEMS	COMPUTATION	GRANT REQUEST TOTAL	MATCHING	TOTAL
Equipment Subtotal				

Budget Narrative: Write out the description of equipment needed and why it is essential for the project.

Write your response:

_____

_____

_____

_____

_____

_____

_____

_____

Grant Request Total: _____

Nonfederal Total: _____

Total Equipment: _____

SUPPLIES

Supplies are where a lot of your items may be listed. This is basically what it sounds like: what supplies will your project need? This can include consumables, such as paper, printing costs, staples, and so forth. It can also include pamphlets and other types of costs.

e.g., Youth Soccer Rocks Supplies items.

SUPPLIES				
TYPES OF SUPPLIES	COMPUTATION	GRANT REQUEST TOTAL	MATCHING	TOTAL
Consumables	Paper, staples, ink, cleaning supplies at $100 per month × 12 months	$600	$600	$1,200
Soccer balls	10 soccer balls at $25 each	$250	$-	$250
Soccer uniforms	110 soccer uniforms at $50 each	$5,500	$-	$5,500
Brochures and pamphlets	$1 × 2000	$-	$2,000	$2,000
Supplies Subtotal		$6,350	$2,600	$8,950

Budget Narrative: Example

Consumables: Youth Rocking Socks requests $600 per year from the grant and will provide a nonfederal match of $600 per year from Rocking Socks Foundation. Consumables include paper, staples, ink, cleaning supplies, and clipboards. Consumables total $1,200 per year.

Soccer balls: Youth Soccer Rocks will purchase 10 soccer balls at $25 each to use in practice and for games, totaling $250.

Soccer uniforms: Youth Soccer Rocks will provide 110 soccer uniforms at $50 each, totaling $5,500 each. Even though we anticipate only 100 youth participants, we will have extra uniforms in case the uniforms are ruined due to the nature of the sport.

Brochures and pamphlets: Youth Soccer Rocks will have 2,000 brochures or pamphlets printed to hand out at community events, schools, soccer games, and other places. These will cost $1 each, totaling $2,000.

Grant Request Total: $6,350

Nonfederal Total: $2,600

Total Supplies: $8,950

Now, your turn.

SUPPLIES				
TYPES OF SUPPLIES	COMPUTATION	GRANT REQUEST TOTAL	MATCHING	TOTAL
Supplies Subtotal				

Budget Narrative: Write out the description for each supply needed and why it is essential for the project.

Write your response:

_____

_____

_____

_____

_____

_____

_____

_____

_____

_____

Grant Request Total: _____

Nonfederal Total: _____

Total Supplies: _____

CONTRACTUAL

"Contractual" refers to the types of services or items that different sources are performing. This, at times, can be where you may contract an accounting agency to do your bookkeeping. If you contract this work out, you would not include the agency as an employee in the personnel category because you are not paying their fringe benefits, and they are not an employee. The example we will use is that Youth Soccer Rocks will hire a contractor to perform two months of advertising for their soccer program to recruit participants. Because Youth Soccer Rocks has a formal contract with the advertising agency, we will include this under contractual.

e.g., Youth Soccer Rocks will hire Rocking Socks Media to conduct advertising for awareness and outreach for recruiting participants.

CONTRACTUAL				
TYPES	COMPUTATION	GRANT REQUEST TOTAL	MATCHING	TOTAL
Advertising	2 months x $1000	$2,000	$0	$2,000
Contractual Subtotal		$2,000	$0	$2,000

Budget Narrative: Example

Advertising: Youth Soccer Rocks will hire an advertising contractor to create public awareness and advertisements on the television and radio for two months at $1,000 for each month, totaling $2,000.

Grant Request Total: $2,000

Nonfederal Total: $0

Total Contractual: $2,000

Now, your turn.

CONTRACTUAL				
TYPES	COMPUTATION	GRANT REQUEST TOTAL	MATCHING	TOTAL
Contractual Subtotal				

Budget Narrative: Write out the description for each contractor or consultant required and why the job is essential for the project.

Write your response:

_____

_____

_____

_____

_____

_____

_____

_____

_____

_____

Grant Request Total: _____

Nonfederal Total: _____

Total Contractual: _____

OTHER

The "Other" category is basically where you put any anticipated expenses not listed elsewhere. I include computers within this category, although those can also be included within "Supplies." If you can tell by now, there are certain black-and-white items in a budget while others are a little gray. This is where we would identify any items that wouldn't be classified in any other category. You will want to work with your finance division to know under what categories they allocate items. That way, it will be clear across all your grant programs.

OTHER				
TYPES	COMPUTATION	GRANT REQUEST TOTAL	MATCHING	TOTAL
Computers	$1,000 × 2 computers	$2,000	$-	$2,000
Room for nutrition classes	150 sq. feet at $100 for 10 sessions	$-	$1,500	$1,500
Internet	$100 per month × 12 months	$600	$600	$1,200
Other Subtotal		$2,600	$2,100	$4,700

Budget Narrative: Example

Computers: Youth Soccer Rocks will purchase two computers—one for the project manager and one for the bookkeeper—to complete all programmatic and financial reports. The computers will be $1,000 each, totaling $2,000.

Venue for Nutrition: Youth Rocking Socks High School will provide a space of 150 square feet valued at $100 per hour for a total of 10 hours (sessions) to discuss nutrition health. The use of this space totals $1,500.

Internet: The Internet will be required for all reports, social media posts, and administration. Internet cost is $100 per month for 12 months, totaling $1,200. We will request $600 from the grant, and $600 will be covered by a nonfederal foundation grant.

Grant Request Total: $2,600

Nonfederal Total: $2,100

Total Other: $4,700

Now, your turn.

OTHER				
TYPES	COMPUTATION	GRANT REQUEST TOTAL	MATCHING	TOTAL
Other Subtotal				

Budget Narrative: Write out the description for anything else needed and why it is essential for the project.

Write your response:

_____

_____

_____

_____

_____

_____

_____

_____

_____

_____

_____

_____

_____

Grant Request Total: _____

Nonfederal Total: _____

Total Other: _____

INDIRECT COSTS

If you have an indirect cost rate, then include what that is. If you do not, I highly recommend that you include the allowed a de minimis indirect cost rate of 10%. You can go into negotiations for a higher amount of an indirect cost rate, but this is a grueling annual process. Plus, if you have a higher indirect cost rate, that means that it will take away from your project budget. The 10% is not too much to come off the top and can help provide support for other costs that may not be included in the project costs as they are indirect. These costs may include executive and administrative salaries (as mentioned in the Personnel section), rent, utilities, and other costs that are more "overhead" appropriate.

e.g., Youth Soccer Rocks will include a de minimis 10% indirect cost rate that will cover costs of utilities, legal fees, insurance, etc.

INDIRECT COST				
INDIRECT COST RATE	COMPUTATION	GRANT REQUEST TOTAL	MATCHING	TOTAL
Indirect	10.00%	$12,312	$1,711	$14,023

Budget Narrative: Example

Indirect Cost: Youth Soccer Rocks will include a de minimis 10% indirect cost rate that will cover costs of utilities, legal fees, insurance, and audits.

Grant Request Total: $12,312.48

Nonfederal Total: $1,710.68

Total Indirect: $14,023.16

Budget Narrative: Write out the indirect cost, and, if it is a negotiated indirect cost rate, attach the negotiated form. If it is a different percentage, include what is included in your indirect costs.

Write your response:

_____

_____

_____

_____

_____

Grant Request Total: _____

Nonfederal Total: _____

Total Indirect: _____

Okay, there is your budget on a line-by-line computation and your budget narrative. Phew.

TOTAL COSTS

Time to add it all up.

Total Costs: Example

Grant Request Total: $135,437

Nonfederal Total: $18,817

Total: $156,855

Your turn:

Grant Request Total: _____

Nonfederal Total: _____

Total: _____

S: STRATEGIC BUDGETS

In Chapter Twelve, you learned how to write a strategic budget and budget narrative in a format that grant reviewers appreciate. You now know in which category to put each item of your budget and how to calculate costs. You also got links to resources to help you put a reliable cost on each item. And you also have some nifty templates available to you!

If the grant is for more than one year, make sure you add in subsequent years. Also, be sure you include any nonfederal matching if it is required and letters of commitment, leases, memorandums of understanding and other required contracts to demonstrate commitment. If you are requesting an item worth more than $5,000, include at least three quotes to demonstrate the cost of the request and to show cost efficiency.

Go to www.grantwritingandfunding.com/bookbonus **for a free downloadable Excel budget worksheet.**

For a full view, see below: Example

PERSONNEL				
POSITION TITLE	COMPUTATION (HOURLY RATE × # OF HOURS)	GRANT REQUEST TOTAL	MATCHING	TOTAL
e.g., Director	($35 per hour × 2080 hours) × 30%	$21,840		$21,840
Project Manager	$25 per hour × 2080 hours	$52,000		$52,000
Coach	$20 per hour × 560 hours		$11,200	$11,200
Bookkeeper	($15 per hour × 1040 hours) × 20%	$3,120		$3,120
Personnel Subtotal	The sum of all personnel	$76,960	$11,200	$88,160

FRINGE BENEFITS

FRINGE BENEFITS	RATE	GRANT REQUEST TOTAL	MATCHING	TOTAL
FICA	Multiply the total of the personnel salary by 7.65%	$5,887	$857	$6,744
Workers Comp	Multiply the total by 1.5%	$1,154	$168	$1,322
Health Insurance	Each full-time person receives $350 per month	$5,460	$-	$5,460
Fringe Benefits Subtotal		$12,502	$1,025	$13,527

TRAVEL

TYPE	COMPUTATION	GRANT REQUEST TOTAL	MATCHING	TOTAL
Conference/ Required Training	Required Grant in D.C. in January			
Airfare	$500 × 2 people	$1,000	$-	$1,000
Lodging	$182 per day for 3 nights for 2 people	$1,092	$-	$1,092
Meals & Incidentals	$69 per day for 3 days for 2 people + $51.75 for two days of traveling	$621	$-	$621
Mileage for Driving for Work	Driving kids to soccer—average 100 miles per week × 52 weeks × $.535 per mile.	$-	$2,782	$2,782
Travel Subtotal	Add up everything	$2,713	$2,782	$5,495

EQUIPMENT

ITEMS	COMPUTATION	GRANT REQUEST TOTAL	MATCHING	TOTAL
One Minivan	Purchasing a minivan	$20,000	$-	$20,000
Equipment Subtotal		$20,000	$-	$20,000

SUPPLIES				
TYPES OF SUPPLIES	COMPUTATION	GRANT REQUEST TOTAL	MATCHING	TOTAL
Consumables	Paper, staples, ink, cleaning supplies at $100 per month × 12 months	$600	$600	$1,200
Soccer balls	10 soccer balls at $25 each	$250	$-	$250
Soccer uniforms	110 soccer uniforms at $50 each	$5,500	$-	$5,500
Brochures and pamphlets	$1 × 2000	$-	$2,000	$2,000
Supplies Subtotal		$6,350	$2,600	$8,950

CONTRACTUAL				
TYPES	COMPUTATION	GRANT REQUEST TOTAL	MATCHING	TOTAL
Advertising	2 months x $1000	$2,000	$0	$2,000
Contractual Subtotal		$2,000	$0	$2,000

OTHER				
TYPES	COMPUTATION	GRANT REQUEST TOTAL	MATCHING	TOTAL
Computers	$1,000 × 2 computers	$2,000	$-	$2,000
Room for nutrition classes	150 sq. feet at $100 for 10 sessions	$-	$1,500	$1,500
Internet	$100 per month × 12 months	$600	$600	$1,200
Other Subtotal		$2,600	$2,100	$4,700

TOTAL DIRECT COSTS				
	COMPUTATION	GRANT REQUEST TOTAL	MATCHING	TOTAL
Direct Costs Subtotal	Add up all subtotals	$123,124	$17,107	$142,832
INDIRECT COST				
INDIRECT COST RATE	COMPUTATION	GRANT REQUEST TOTAL	MATCHING	TOTAL
Indirect	10.00%	$12,312	$1,711	$14,023
TOTAL COSTS	Add up Direct Costs with Indirect Cost	$135,437	$18,817	$156,855

Now, your turn.

BUDGET LINE BY LINE WORKSHEET				
PERSONNEL				
POSITION TITLE	COMPUTATION (HOURLY RATE × # OF HOURS)	GRANT REQUEST TOTAL	MATCHING	TOTAL
Personnel Subtotal	The sum of all personnel			
FRINGE BENEFITS				
FRINGE BENEFITS	RATE	GRANT REQUEST TOTAL	MATCHING	TOTAL
FICA	Multiply the total of the personnel salary by 7.65%			
Unemployment				
Workers Comp				
Retirement				
Health Insurance				
Fringe Benefits Subtotal				

TRAVEL*

TYPE	COMPUTATION	GRANT REQUEST TOTAL	MATCHING	TOTAL
Conference/ Required Training	Name of training:			
Airfare	Cost of flight × number of individuals			
Lodging	Costs of hotel × number of nights × number of people			
Meals & Incidentals	Daily per diem rate × number of days × number of people			
Mileage for Driving for Work	Daily rental car costs × number of days × number of people			
Travel Subtotal	Add up everything			

EQUIPMENT

ITEMS	COMPUTATION	GRANT REQUEST TOTAL	MATCHING	TOTAL
Equipment Subtotal				

SUPPLIES

TYPES OF SUPPLIES	COMPUTATION	GRANT REQUEST TOTAL	MATCHING	TOTAL
Supplies Subtotal				

CONTRACTUAL				
TYPES	COMPUTATION	GRANT REQUEST TOTAL	MATCHING	TOTAL
Contractual Subtotal				

OTHER				
TYPES	COMPUTATION	GRANT REQUEST TOTAL	MATCHING	TOTAL
Other Subtotal				

TOTAL DIRECT COSTS				
	COMPUTATION	GRANT REQUEST TOTAL	MATCHING	TOTAL
Direct Costs Subtotal	Add up all subtotals			

INDIRECT COST				
INDIRECT COST RATE	COMPUTATION	GRANT REQUEST TOTAL	MATCHING	TOTAL
Indirect				
TOTAL COSTS	Add up Direct Costs with Indirect Cost			

"If you can't explain it simply, you don't understand it well enough."

~ ALBERT EINSTEIN

TIPS

✓ Your budget should be S.M.A.R.T., just like your objectives.

✓ You will get many different resume formats from employees. One tip is to give them each a template and keep it to no more than two pages. Sometimes, resumes are not included in page counts for grants, but sometimes, they are. Plus, you want to keep the resumes super easy for grant reviewers to look at and find specific experience that relates to your project or the roles that employees will have in the grant project.

TOOLS

✓ Use your timeline plan as a guide when writing out your budget to ensure all items are included in both your timeline (from your budget) and your budget (from your timeline).

✓ Visit https://www.dol.gov/whd/ for more information for your specific state's wages.

✓ You can easily visit https://www.gsa.gov/portal/content/104877 to get the meals and incidentals rates and lodging for virtually every city in the United States.

✓ Visit the IRS website for updated mileage rates information: https://www.irs.gov/newsroom/irs-issues-standard-mileage-rates-for-2019#targetText=Beginning%20on%20Jan.%201%2C%202019,the%20rate%20for%202018%2C%20and.

TEMPLATES

✓ For a downloadable template of of a line-by-line budget, visit www.grantwritingandfunding.com/bookbonus.

NOTES:

SECTION 3:
PUTTING IT TOGETHER

CHAPTER THIRTEEN
PROJECT NARRATIVE

In this chapter, you will learn how to write the (drum roll, please) project design. We will go over how to list out the activities for the project, the selection process, where the project will take place, the challenges, the contingencies, the sustainability plan, nonfederal partners and resources, and leveraged resources and what you need in place to oversee and monitor nonfederal resources and partners. This is where a lot of people start writing, but—as you should be able to tell by now—if you start writing here, you may rewrite this several times. Why? Well, if you do not understand your true problem, have an overarching goal, have clear objectives and outcomes, and know what your budget can cover…then, yes, you will be just coming up with ideas for the project approach. This can turn into a crazy process where grants really do feel too overwhelming. This might be where you have always started and then proceeded to tear at hair and gain 10 pounds. I get this. But I have also shown you how to prevent this in the previous chapters. Don't start with project design!

If you have followed this guide, you have done the following *already:*

- Read the FOA or RFP
- Completed research and have backed up needs with current references and have identified a target population
- Identified a goal and developed S.M.A.R.T. objectives, specific outcomes, and a tasked timeline
- Finalized a budget to include identifying resources for any matching funds required

In this way, the project design can be put together very easily. You should be able to get the information through emails or phone calls instead of at panicked grant meetings where things will go all wrong! That being said, don't leave this part for the day before a grant is due thinking it is a piece of cake. You still must write this section and make sure you have all the information for the details.

Often, this section also has a lot of points attached to it. As mentioned previously, sometimes, parts of the other sections are included in the project design. Get those parts of the project design completed first if they are solely listed in the project design (also called project approach, about the project, project narrative, etc.).

What are detailed descriptions of all activities? Use your action plan timeline as a guide to write each activity in clear sentences, and include additional information to include all aspects of the activity.

e.g., The kickoff meeting will include the executive director and board of directors, and we will look over all objectives, goals, and activities. We will immediately start on grant implementation.

Now, you write your response:

_____

_____

_____

_____

_____

_____

_____

_____

_____

_____

_____

_____

How will you select beneficiaries/clients/etc.?

e.g., Youth Soccer Rocks will utilize applications with the highest poverty threshold household youth to be prioritized.

Now, you write your response:

_____

_____

_____

_____

_____

_____

_____

_____

_____

_____

_____

_____

_____

Where will your project take place?

e.g., Youth Soccer Rocks activities will occur at the Clubhouse soccer pitch, and classes will be held at Rocking Socks High School. Our main headquarters will be at the Youth Soccer Rocks suite where we have one office of 200 square feet.

Now, you write your response:

_____

_____

_____

_____

_____

_____

_____

CHALLENGES, CONTINGENCIES, AND SUSTAINABILITY

Challenges, contingencies, and sustainability plans are important to identify in your project design. Challenges are what could go wrong, contingencies are what will be put in place to mitigate challenges, and sustainability plans are how the project can be maintained after the grant has ended. These components are important to look at because you will face challenges when administering a grant. Things will come up, and sometimes, you can be ahead of the curve by identifying some potential issues and outlining a plan to address them. Businesses do this within business plans, but somehow, the world of nonprofits tends to overlook this important process. The reality is that things do happen, so you need to be prepared to work through the hiccups and bumps or derailments to implement someone else's money. Plus, let's face it, this money is going to end. Grants are kind of like startup capital or seed money. Once the grant is over, the funding source wants to know that the project will still operate at some level.

Flashback to your goal: What change are you going to make in your community? This will be a lasting change and positively impact your community. If the grant project just fades out as soon as the money is gone, then what real impact have you had? This is another reason so many grants require matching nonfederal funds. They want to know that the community is supporting the project.

Challenges: What could go wrong?

Contingency: What will you put in place to mitigate challenges?

Sustainability Plans: How can the project keep going when the grant has ended?

What are your potential challenges?

e.g., Not enough youth will sign up for the Youth Soccer Rocks club.

Now, you write your response:

_____

_____

_____

_____

_____

_____

_____

_____

_____

_____

What are your contingencies?

e.g., We will work with our partners to increase referrals and increase our visits to more schools. We are confident the incentives of scholarships, trips away from home to games, free uniforms, health checks, and the nutrition program will attract more than 100 disadvantaged youth.

Now, you write your response:

_____

_____

_____

_____

_____

_____

_____

_____

_____

_____

What is your sustainability plan?

e.g., Youth Soccer Rocks will leverage business partners, rotary clubs, and other partners with continued sponsorship of scholarships. We will also have fundraisers, such as car washes and other events, whereby the youth will be significant contributors to raise money for the second-year scholarships.

Now, you write your response:

_____

_____

_____

_____

_____

_____

_____

_____

_____

_____

NONFEDERAL FUNDS

This may seem like a budget section, but if nonfederal funds are required as a match for your grant, this is also shown in the project design. Of course, this also needs to be demonstrated within the budget; you will identify where your nonfederal support comes from within the project design. Specifically, you must point out what type of nonfederal support your organization has secured, any other leveraged funds, and how the partnership will be secured. A reminder is that nonfederal funds must be from nonfederal resources and may be a hard or soft match, dependent on the FOA. If there is no requirement for nonfederal matching, I would only include any support as "leveraging." Although the difference sounds only semantic, there is a difference in the level of support. Also, if the grant only requires a 20% nonfederal match, don't state that you will match 50% and think that will get you brownie points. It may show more support, but you will be required to give that 50% since you stated you would—even though the grant did not originally require that much of a match. That can deduct brownie points because the reviewers know that things happen (remember back to challenges and contingencies), and they know that one of your funding sources might drop off and leave you scrambling.

Who are some of your nonfederal resources? (in-kind volunteers, venue space, vehicles, other nonfederal grants, etc.)

e.g., Youth Soccer Rocks will have the in-kind support of Rocking Socks High School for a space to teach our nutrition classes valued at $150 per class for 10 classes per year with a total value of $1,500. See attached letter of commitment. These are state (nonfederal) monies.

Now, you write your response:

_____

_____

_____

_____

_____

_____

_____

_____

_____

What are leveraged resources? (These may be other federal grants or programs that cannot add a monetary value to your budget but can add value of support).

e.g., Youth Soccer Rocks will have our headquarters in a federal building that is leveraged space of 200 square feet at no cost.

Now, you write your response:

_____

_____

_____

_____

_____

_____

_____

_____

_____

_____

_____

_____

How will you get these nonfederal and leveraged sources?

e.g., Youth Soccer Rocks will identify our partners at our next meetings. The project assistant will communicate via email messages to request letters of support. We will obtain signed letters of commitment and support with all monetary value listed in the letters. We will do fundraising to secure any other outstanding matching funding.

Now, you write your response:

_____

_____

_____

_____

_____

_____

_____

_____

_____

_____

_____

_____

How will you oversee and monitor all your nonfederal resources and partnerships?

e.g., Youth Soccer Rocks will meet with our partners monthly and request reports for our meetings to outline all responsibilities.

Now, you write your response:

_____

_____

_____

_____

_____

_____

_____

_____

_____

_____

_____

_____

_____

PROJECT NARRATIVE

So, there you have it. Once you have all other measures in place, go to town writing your project approach. Make sure you leave ample time to write this section. At times, some funding sources request logic models, detailed training plans, evaluation plans, and so forth. I am not covering all of those items in this book (otherwise, it would have the overwhelming "thud" factor, and you may never even open it to do more than smell the newly printed pages and then put it on your shelf to look smart), but I will include an explanation of these items—and possibly more templates—on my podcast and website.

In Chapter Thirteen, you learned how to write a detailed account of the following:

- Activities
- Selection process
- Location
- Challenges, contingencies, and sustainability plan
- Nonfederal partners and resources
- Leveraged resources
- Overseeing and monitoring nonfederal resources and partners

These elements will help frame your project design.

TIPS

✓ When writing a grant, do not start with the project design!

✓ Make sure to include challenges, contingencies, and sustainability plans.

TOOLS

✓ Use your timeline plan as a guide when writing out your project narrative.

TEMPLATES

✓ For a downloadable template of a letter of support, visit www.grantwritingandfunding.com/bookbonus.

NOTES:

CHAPTER FOURTEEN

ABOUT THE ORGANIZATION

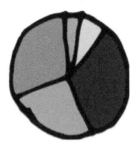

This section is pretty self-explanatory, but you would be surprised how many organizations do not have this information in one easily accessible location. Chances are—since you have bought this workbook—you are in one of those organizations. You do not have to be in one of those organizations any longer! Now is your turn to go from pulling your hair out/gaining five pounds of chocolate weight to a very organized, click-on-one-button or open-to-this-chapter and *voila!* situation.

You might be tempted to jump over this part, thinking, "Yeah, I got this information listed somewhere." That's great if you have it, but even so, don't skip this section. Instead, go ahead and find all this information (as it probably is not listed all in one easy-to-find place but might be scattered in different folders) and then write it down and put it in one electronic folder called "Administration". If you are a freelance grant writer, then you should have an "Administration" folder for each of your clients. Make sure you ask them for all of the information listed in the section as soon as you sign a contract with them, even before you start writing grants.

Make notes or highlight the sections you do not have, and write it all in your planner to follow up with human resources, the program manager, or executive director. Do it within the next week so you can have this section completed. You want to be prepared when that grant comes up…which will usually be at the most inconvenient time, *i.e., Here's the perfect grant, but it's due in two weeks!*

Funding sources want to know about your organization. They want to know that your organization is credible, has adequate staffing and processes to implement the grant, and is fiscally responsible. They basically want to get a good idea of who you are and what you stand for so that, if awarded, you can manage the grant. In this chapter, we are going to outline how to organize all this information so you can best be prepared to win that grant. I will show you a way to keep track of all the following:

1. Status of your organization

2. Your vision

3. Activities your organization has completed

4. Other grants or funding your organization has received

5. Board officers and members
6. Staffing
7. Staffing structure
8. Financial oversight and management of funds
9. Job roles for projects
10. Partners

When was your organization founded and by whom?

e.g., Youth Soccer Rocks was founded in 2017 by Jane Doe and was incorporated as an IRS tax-exempt 501(c)3 nonprofit organization in 2018.

Now, you write your response:

_____

_____

_____

_____

_____

_____

_____

_____

Why was your organization founded (i.e., Write your mission statement)?

e.g., Youth Soccer Rocks has a mission to provide sports activities for youth..

Now, you write your response:

_____

_____

_____

_____

_____

_____

_____

_____

_____

What are some similar activities/projects that your organization has successfully accomplished?

e.g., Youth Soccer Rocks partnered with Rocking Health to provide health screenings for 300 youth athletes in 2018.

Now, you write your response:

_____

_____

_____

_____

_____

_____

_____

What are other grants that your organization has received, from whom, for what, how much, and in what year?

For an electronic template, visit www.grantwritingandfunding.com/bookbonus.

GRANT (FROM WHOM?)	TYPE OF FUNDING	HOW MUCH?	YEAR AWARDED
Rocking Socks Foundation	Soccer Uniforms	$20,000	2018
Rocking Socks Public Health	Nutrition Education	$5,000	Annually, since 2013

Now, you write your response:

GRANT (FROM WHOM?)	TYPE OF FUNDING	HOW MUCH?	YEAR AWARDED

Who is on your board of directors? Provide a bio for each board member.

For a board member template, visit www.grantwritingandfunding.com/bookbonus.

e.g., See below.

BOARD OFFICER SEAT	NAME	TITLE	PHONE NUMBER	EMAIL	SHORT BIO
Chair	Jane Doe	CEO	(XXX) XXX-XXXX	janedoe@ rockingsocks.com	Former soccer champion of the entire Rocking Socks region, now CEO of Soccer Rocks
Vice Chair	Joe Schmo				Has been playing soccer all his life and works at a hardware store
Secretary	Jay Pitch				Former beneficiary of Youth Soccer Rocks and volunteers as a soccer coach
Treasurer	Judith Goal				CPA at Rocking Socks Accounting Firm
Committee Chair	Jean Kicks				Physical Education teacher at Rocking Socks High School
Member	Joan Punt				Legal advisor
Member	Jeff Cross				Parent of current beneficiary at Youth Soccer Rocks

Now, your turn:

BOARD OFFICER SEAT	NAME	TITLE	PHONE NUMBER	EMAIL	SHORT BIO

Who are your staff members, and what is their employment status (full-time, part-time, volunteer, etc.)?Provide a short bio for each staff member.

For an employee and staff template, please visit www.grantwritingandfunding.com/bookbonus.

TITLE	NAME	EMPLOYMENT TYPE	SHORT BIO
Executive Director	Janice Doe	Full-time employee	Janice has a master's degree in sports psychology and has been at Youth Soccer Rocks since 2011.
Project Coordinator	Emily Wise	Full-time employee	Emily has a bachelor's degree in sociology and has been at Youth Soccer Rocks since 2014.
Coach	Barry Wise	Part-time employee	Barry has a bachelor's degree in sports and has been at Youth Soccer Rocks since 2014.
Accountant	Emma Jones	Part-time employee	Emma is a CPA and has been at Youth Soccer Rocks since 2015.

Now, you write your response:

TITLE	NAME	EMPLOYMENT TYPE	SHORT BIO

Do you have a resume and job description for each staff member? (Check one)

Yes _____ No _____ Not Sure _____

If you are not sure, then you need to find out. This is usually something human resources can help you with. If you do have resumes, make sure that they are updated each year. Yes, even if the coach has been the coach for three years. Why? Well, the experience, education, certificates, and so forth usually increase every year. There are so many trainings and conferences that your staff may attend, but they do not always include those certificates in their resume. These are extremely useful for various reasons.

The coach may have attended several conferences for the impact of sports and disadvantaged youth while working at Youth Soccer Rocks. If you only have the coach's resume that he/she submitted before he/she started working at Youth Soccer Rocks and he/she had never worked with disadvantaged youth, then you could lose points on a grant application. How? Well, if one criterion from a grant application is "Demonstrate how your staff has the qualifications to work with your disadvantaged youth," and you just attach the old resume of the coach, you are not demonstrating anything of value. A reviewer will go through that resume and not identify any direct training or experience and may not award you points. So, make sure all staff update their resumes annually!

Once you have received all updated resumes, put them into a folder: **Master Grant Information.**

What is your staffing structure (who reports to whom?)?

e.g., Youth Soccer Rocks has the following staffing structure: The board of directors meets quarterly and oversees all projects. The executive director reports to the board and oversees all staff at weekly meetings. The project coordinator has the key responsibilities of outreach, networking, and implementing all project activities. The coach organizes all youth activities. The bookkeeper maintains all financial books.

Now, you write your response:

What is your financial plan for oversight and management of funds?

e.g., Youth Soccer Rocks has a robust background in grant management, both federal and nonfederal, and has a sound reporting and accounting system in place.

Now, you write your response:

If you want to be very precise and are working on a particular project or grant, answer the following questions:

What are the job roles for the project? Who will you hire?

e.g., The Project Director and Youth Coach are two primary positions. These individuals currently volunteer for Youth Soccer Rocks and have submitted letters of commitment to this project. Both staff members will be hired within the first month of the project by the board of directors. (Refer to Attachment A for commitment letters and resumes.)

Now, you write your response:

_____

_____

_____

_____

_____

_____

_____

_____

_____

Who are your partners for this specific project?

e.g., Include signed and dated letters of support, letters of commitment, letters of testimony, or memorandums of understanding with appropriate partners. Also, put any values of commitment in these letters so you can also use them as nonfederal match letters of leveraged support.

Now, you write your response:

_____

_____

_____

_____

_____

_____

_____

_____

_____

_____

_____

List all partners and what their involvement is in short form within the narrative:

e.g., All matching is from a nonfederal foundation grant from the Rocking Socks Sports Foundation and totals $17,607 (rounded to the nearest dollar amount). A coach will volunteer at $20 per hour for 560 hours at $11,200 with FICA at $856.80 and Workers Comp Multiply at $168.00. Mileage for driving the soccer participants to games will average at 100 miles per week multiplied by 52 weeks and at $ .535 per mile, totaling $2,782. Consumables will be provided and include paper, staples, ink, cleaning supplies at $100 per month multiplied by 12 months, totaling $1200. Brochures and pamphlets for outreach and awareness of the soccer project will total $2,000.

Now, you write your response:

ABOUT THE ORGANIZATION

It is always important to keep your organization information up to date and accessible. This may be one of the most underperformed areas of an organization while also being the most basic. It can be confusing for funding sources to get a mix of outdated information. For example, if a newspaper suddenly reaches out to a project manager and requests information about your organization (because they are doing a feature on soccer organizations), but that project manager has no idea where all the information is, then it can be troubling. More critically, it is problematic if you are writing a grant, and it takes you days or weeks to gather this information as the people you emailed do not see it as a priority.

In this chapter, you learned what information is most critical to keep accessible, and you were given templates and structures for how to keep this information. As a grant writer (or when you are acting in the capacity of a grant writer), make sure you annually update staff resumes, board members and their bios, partners, grants, financial policies and procedures, and other pertinent information. Specifically, you learned how to best keep track of the following:

1. Status of your organization
2. Your vision
3. Activities your organization has completed
4. Other grants or funding your organization has received
5. Board officers and members
6. Staffing
7. Staffing structure
8. Financial oversight and management of funds
9. Job roles for projects
10. Partners

As an extra section, I will add an area to keep important information in this workbook. Just be sure to keep this book in a safe place!

I will not go into depth on what these numbers stand for, but you will need them if you are submitting for grants. I will cover these numbers in a different book, but keep these numbers handy!

Employment Identification Number (EIN): A unique identification number that is assigned to a business entity so that they can easily be identified by the Internal Revenue Service. https://www.irs.gov/businesses/small-businesses-self-employed/apply-for-an-employer-identification-number-ein-online

EIN: _____

Username: _____

Password: _____

Other: _____

Data Universal Numbering System (DUNS): A nine-digit number that uniquely identifies a business. http://www.dnb.com/

DUNS: _____

Username: _____

Password: _____

Other: _____

System for Award Management (SAM): A number assigned by the federal government to access federal monies. https://www.sam.gov/portal/SAM/##11

SAM: _____

Username: _____

Password: _____

Other: _____

Place for other numbers and grant information:

_____

_____

_____

_____

_____

_____

_____

_____

_____

_____

_____

_____

_____

TIPS

✓ You want to be prepared when that grant comes up—which it will and at the most inconvenient time.

✓ Funding sources want to get a good idea of who you are and what you stand for so, if awarded, you can manage the grant.

✓ Make sure all staff update their resumes annually!

TOOLS

✓ See templates.

TEMPLATES

✓ To get a downloadable template to keep track of your grants, visit www.grantwritingandfunding.com/bookbonus.

✓ For a downloadable template for your board of directors, visit www.grantwritingandfunding.com/bookbonus.

✓ For a downloadable template for your staff, visit www.grantwritingandfunding.com/bookbonus.

NOTES:

CHAPTER FIFTEEN

CONCLUSION

Thank you for joining me on this journey. You should now have a clear framework for what the grant-writing process is and how to write a winning grant! Grants have gotten the rep of being super technical and tremendously difficult to write. Through these tips, tools, and templates, you should be well on your way to writing a competitive grant. This book should have helped reduce your level of stress associated with writing a grant, eliminated the more technical parts, and made grant writing a whole LOT easier.

I wrote this book to be **helpful** and to be written in and utilized. I hope your book is now underlined, highlighted, marked up, and scuffed up and has coffee stains (or wine stains). Send me an email if you have a question, or follow my podcast or blog. If you do send me a question, I will try my best to even answer it via podcast. Because, if you have a certain question, there are probably many others who have the same question.

You have now learned about the following items:

- the mindset behind grants
- the myths and truths of grants
- different types of grants
- how to think about grants

You also now have a framework (including downloadables!) on the following:

- the G.R.A.N.T.S. formula
- how to write a project narrative
- how to construct "about your organization"

I wrote this book after perusing the market and seeing that there were only academia-friendly grant-writing books, and I thought zzzzzz…I mean, *Wow*, there needs to be something simpler. The whole reason people are buying grant-writing books is to learn how to write a grant—not get a degree in grant writing.

I hope you enjoyed this book, and—more importantly—I hope that the tips, tools, templates, and quirky humor help you get grants awarded! I treasure emails that also talk about how any training has helped your organization get funding.

CHAPTER SIXTEEN

RESOURCES

Please see a list of the following resources on grant-related information.

Some places to find grants:

- https://www.grants.gov
- Agency Websites
- Foundations
- Foundation Directory
- UN and International
- Grant Consulting Companies

Other Information:

Form: 1023 https://www.irs.gov/uac/about-form-1023

Form 1023 EZ: https://www.irs.gov/uac/about-form-1023ez

EIN: https://www.irs.gov/businesses/small-businesses-self-employed/apply-for-an-employer-identification-number-ein-online

DUNS: http://www.dnb.com/

SAM: https://www.sam.gov/sam/SAM_Guide/SAM_User_Guide.htm#_Toc330768937 https://www.sam.gov/portal/SAM/##11

Conflict of Interest Policy Sample: http://www.mtnonprofit.org/uploadedFiles/Files/ About/Conflict_of_Interest_Policy_and_Statement.pdf

Financial Policies & Procedures: http://ccaonline.com.au/financial-policy-procedures -manual-essential-business/

GuideStar: https://www.guidestar.org/Home.aspx

OMB Super Circular: Regulations https://www.gpo.gov/fdsys/pkg/FR-2013-12-26/ pdf/2013-30465.pdf

Agency websites

Foundation Directory: https://fconline.foundationcenter.org

Here-4-You Consulting (Faith-based foundations): https://www.npfunds.com/christian-funding-directory/

Local Newspaper, Internet, U.S. Census, etc.

Grant Writing & Funding (sometimes we publish grant opportunities!) www.grantwritingandfunding.com

Grant Writing & Funding podcast on SoundCloud or iTunes

QUICK FAVOR

Thank you so much for reading this book. I hope that it now has coffee stains and is thoroughly marked up. May I ask a quick favor?

Will you take a moment to leave an honest review for this book on Amazon? Reviews are the absolute best way to help others find out about this book and, hopefully, help increase their funding for their organization! You can just go to Amazon and type in this title and leave a review!

Also, I would LOVE to hear from you. Please let me know how this book has helped your organization and what other information on grants you would like to know.

Okay, that wraps it up. Go win some grant awards!

For more information about Grant Writing & Funding and Holly, visit

Web: www.grantwritingandfunding.com

Email: holly@grantwritingandfunding.com

Facebook: @grantwritingandfunding

Instagram: @hollyrustick

iTunes: Grant Writing & Funding Podcast

YouTube: Grant Writing & Funding

Want to book Holly to speak at your conference or event?

Email: holly@grantwritingandfunding.com

ACKNOWLEDGMENTS

This book is revised, updated, expanded, and retitled! This support (and recommendation!) was given to me by my coach Honorée Corder, the amazing author who inspired me to write this book through her own book. Furthermore, I want to thank all the people who purchased the first book, *Wish Granted! Tips, Tools, & Templates to Write a Winning Grant!* You have inspired me to continue to provide value and skills to more and more people. If no one was reading this book, it would be awfully boring writing another version! I'd also like to thank different universities who utilize this book for their curriculum. Thank you, too, to all the Grant Writing & Funding Changemaker Members and podcast listeners who continually inspire me with their grant-writing and funding questions to help advance this book. Of course, I'd also like to thank people who were instrumental in the first version as, without that version, there probably wouldn't be this book! These include the following amazing people: Deborah Ellen, who edited this monster; Susan White, my grant guru and mentor; Jason Salas, the poor guy who reads all the first drafts; Leone Rohr, my one hundred percent foundation freedom mentor; Michelle Rohr, my one hundred dollar mastermind mentor; Hilary Gunning for editing this specific version and dealing with the crazy formatting; Amber Word, the wonderful lady who pushed me to get creative with my expertise; Claudia Lamparzyk, the creative woman who also pushed me forward in this project; Meg Tyquiengco, another fantastic lady who told me to help others with my grant writing; my Empire Mastermind Builder group, for inspiring me and helping with all the idiosyncrasies; my friends and family who believe in me; Tim Grahl, for helping me with the launch and believing in my business; all of you out there who are passionate about your nonprofits and always ask for tips; and, most of all, my daughter, Isabella, who always motivates me to leave a legacy. I love you all.

Made in the USA
Middletown, DE
12 August 2021